The Modern Impulse of
Traditional Judaism

The Modern Impulse of Traditional Judaism

By
ZVI KURZWEIL

Foreword By
NORMAN LAMM

KTAV PUBLISHING HOUSE, INC.
HOBOKEN, NEW JERSEY

Library of Congress Cataloging in Publication Data

Kurzweil, Zvi.
　The modern impulse of traditional Judaism.

　Bibliography: p.
　Includes index.
　　1. Judaism—History—Modern period, 1750-　　—Ad-
dresses, essays, lectures.　2. Orthodox Judaism—
History—Addresses, essays, lectures.　I. Title.
BM195.K88　1985　　296'.09'03　　84-28892
ISBN 0-88125-068-6

Manufactured in the United States of America

To Rose Kushner
in gratitude.

CONTENTS

Foreword

Orthodox Judaism is an "in" topic nowadays. Respectable journalists devote major reports to it, sociologists analyze it, learned societies invite scholarly papers on it. A movement that, fifteen years after the start of this century, was widely expected to fade away and become a relic of interest only to historians and antiquarians, is, fifteen years before the end of this century, full of life, vigor, dynamism—and problems.

The problems largely center on the nature of the Orthodoxy or Orthodoxies that are emerging and their relations to each other. None of them has yet received adequate scholarly attention. The proliferation of "right wing" yeshivot and communities has not been sufficiently documented and, certainly, we do not possess enough competent analysis of this phenomenon. The few articles and works that have appeared are only a beginning, especially if one excludes polemics and apologetics.

The story is no different with Modern or Centrist Orthodoxy (the labels are notoriously short-lived and singularly insignificant). Those of us engaged in the enterprise of leading it, fashioning it, teaching it, and elaborating it are too preoccupied, and lack the proper perspective, to see it in its historical setting and to appreciate the continuities and discontinuities in its development.

It has remained, therefore, to an Israeli scholar familiar with the European antecedents of the modernist wing of Orthodoxy to lay bare the background and thus illuminate the foreground of contemporary centrist Orthodoxy. Zvi Kurzweil makes no pretenses to comprehensiveness. He could hardly do so for a movement which is very much in flux and which requires not only theological but social historians as well to do it justice.

Our author's goals are limited to the ideological roots of the modern impulse in traditional Judaism. This he has done in both a competent and interesting manner, one that will engage the attention of both scholar and layman. Unquestionably, there will be those who will challenge him on this or that point, or wish to add or subtract one item or another from his description. No matter; he has made a beginning, an excellent beginning, in systematically bringing together much of the relevant material. His scholarship is evident throughout this book.

All those who are interested in the contemporary Jewish religious scene, and especially that of Orthodox Judaism, will remain very much in his debt.

HANUKKAH 5745   NORMAN LAMM

Preface

The term "Neo-Orthodoxy," which can be equated with "modern Orthodoxy," was first coined by Max Wiener in his book *Jüdische Religion im Zeitalter der Emanzipation* (Berlin, 1933). He used it to characterize the conception of Judaism developed by Samson Raphael Hirsch and his followers, as distinct from that of the Orthodox Jews of the pre-Emancipation era. Although Wiener must have been aware of the sociological differences involved in the two types, primarily he was concerned with differences of an ideological nature. In the pre-Emancipation era the majority of Jews had accepted their faith and way of life as a matter of course, as a life-style not to be questioned. After the Emancipation this was no longer so. Even among those who remained faithful to Torah Judaism, the quest for the meaning of and justification for its most essential feature, religious precepts, grew in importance. Wiener discerns in Hirsch a strong emotional identification with the commandments and injunctions inherent in the Torah, the scrupulous observance of which was in Hirsch's opinion conducive to the emergence of an ideal humanity, and it was this that led him to develop a new philosophic interpretation for them. It is in this light that Hirsch's work on the symbolism of mitzvot, elaborated both in his commentary to the Pentateuch and in a series of essays, should be seen.

Today, fifty years after the publication of Wiener's book, the modern impulse of traditional Judaism displays additional distinctive features besides those he pointed out, and they are the subject of this essay.

It is not only the need to reinterpret Torah commandments so that they should be comprehensible to contemporary Jewry. Yitzhak Heinemann in his two-volume study on this subject shows that the search for *ta'amei ha-mitzvot*, the rationale for religious commandments, has been a perennial feature of Jewish religious history from rabbinic times, throughout the Middle Ages, down to the present. If the term "Neo-Orthodoxy," resulting from what I call the "modern impulse," is to be applied meaningfully, it should surely convey, in the first place, the conception of an open Judaism, tenets of which may be related to general culture, hospitable to the human arts and sciences and the spirit of man in its widest sense. In actual life this attitude of openness is expressed by the readiness of Orthodox Jews to enter all walks of life and participate in the scientific and technological endeavors of humanity without sacrificing any essential feature of traditional Judaism in the process. This view of Judaism as open, capable of combining with certain manifestations of the human spirit at large, is of fundamental importance, and many of the additional facets of modernity, spelled out in the present essay, flow from it.

Obviously, openness of mind stands in contradiction to dogmatism. Modern traditionalism does not view Judaism as burdened by a dogmatic theology. While it has to admit the existence of fundamental principles of faith, it maintains that their number and interpretation are subject to a legitimate divergence of opinion. This controversy about the principles of faith has not been resolved by an authoritative promulgation of a definitive doctrine of faith to be accepted by all. There is more than a grain of truth in Leon Roth's dictum that Judaism's only dogma is its dogmalessness.

The impact of modernity on traditional Judaism also expresses itself in the attempt to bring out the flexible nature of Halakhah and to substantiate the possibility of its application to all situations of life. Here the work of Eliezer Berkovits is most relevant. In his essay "The Nature and Function of *Halakhah*," in both the Hebrew and English versions, he has gathered together an impressive number of immanent halakhic principles from talmudic and post-talmudic sources testifying to the "wisdom of Torah implementation in the daily life of the Jewish people" and thus disproving the widespread prejudice that Halakhah is in a state of stagnation, incapable of application to modern life situations. The modernist tendencies inherent in the important work of

Menachem Elon on Jewish law and in the legal treatises of Ze'ev Falk deserve special treatment, but go beyond the scope of the present essay.

Yeshayahu Leibovitz's Jewish philosophy is regarded by some observers as being sui generis and not necessarily Orthodox, in either the old or modern sense of the term. I personally find it very relevant to the subject of a modern interpretation of traditional Judaism and characterize it as "traditional Judaism in modern garb." Running through all his writings is his internalization of the spirit of modernity and its absorption into his philosophical thought. His central ideas about Judaism tacitly assimilate the spirit of modern science and philosophy, forestalling, as the Hebrew saying has it, the malaise (objections to these ideas stemming from the spirit of modern science) by its remedy. As he is the boldest innovator in the realm of traditional Judaism, it is little wonder that the main theses of his philosophy have remained controversial. For obvious reasons I have left his political opinions out of account.

I hope I do not have to apologize for the pervasively critical attitude of this essay. Tempered and well-founded criticism does not necessarily detract from the quality of creative work. This applies particularly to the work of the late Isaac Breuer, who must undoubtedly be regarded as one of the builders of Neo-Orthodoxy, though a critical approach to his philosophy is justified.

My detailed treatment of the problem of state and religion calls for comment. In Israel dissatisfaction with the present state of affairs on this issue serves as at least one shibboleth for diagnosing a modern impulse in traditional Jewish thought. The reader will note that even within Neo-Orthodoxy three somewhat different attitudes to this subject are presented (Berkovits, Leibowitz, Kurzweil), and I am surprised to find that my own viewpoint is prima facie the most cautiously conservative of the three.

I should like to thank the editors of the *Radday Festschrift*, published by the Department of General Studies of the Technion, for permission to reprint the chapter on Mendelssohn; the editors of *Tradition* and *Judaism* for permission to use the chapter on Rabbi S. R. Hirsch and on universalism in the philosophy of Rabbi Soloveitchik; to the editor of the *Jerusalem Post*, where shortened versions of the chapters on tolerance according to the teaching of Rabbi A. I. Hacohen Kook and the philosophy of Y. Leibowitz, under the title "State and Religion," have appeared.

My thanks are also due to Rose Kushner and Selma Rabbinowitz for many stylistic suggestions and to Tova Shimron for her patience in typing the manuscript.

Z'vi Kurzweil

Founders of Neo-Orthodoxy

1

Moses Mendelssohn's Conception of Judaism

In writing his treatise *Jerusalem*, Moses Mendelssohn intended to justify from moral, legal, and political viewpoints the right of the Jewish minorities in Central Europe to equal civil status with the indigenous non-Jewish population. However, there may also have been a tacit personal motive in writing the treatise. Since he had established his reputation as a philosopher of the Enlightenment, a champion of freedom of thought, and an opponent of the practice of ecclesiastical power, his non-Jewish contemporaries could not understand his unfailing loyalty to Judaism, which in Christian eyes seemed incongruous with the enlightened views expressed by the philosopher Mendelssohn. The question why he never relinquished Judaism and adopted Christianity was put to him twice, once by Johann Caspar Lavater, and then by August Friedrich Cranz, both of whom were Mendelssohn's contemporaries. In view of the personal implication of Mendelssohn in this issue and his standing as the principal exponent of Judaism of his time, the reader can discern between the lines of careful philosophical argumentation an element of tension rarely absent from a public debate of such significance.

The legal and philosophical basis for his demand for civil rights for the Jews was simple enough. It was rooted in an assumption that must have appeared reasonable to the intelligentsia of the time. It must be borne in mind that his generation was nurtured intellectually by the ideas characteristic of the Age of Enlightenment, i.e., that man is essentially a rational being, no matter what his religious allegiance or ethnic origin might be. Every human being carries within him the natural light of reason, which enables him to shape his decisions, his actions, and in fact his whole life on rational principles. Thus, the central idea of the Age of the Enlightenment contains a universal element, which by its very nature blurs the distinction and dividing lines between various religious and ethnic groups. *Sapere aude*—i.e., "have the audacity to think for yourself"—in these two words did the German philosopher Immanuel Kant sum up the spirit of the Age of Enlightenment.

The intellectual climate of the Age of Enlightenment was naturally favorable to the inclusion of Jews as equal members of the general body of the Prussian king's subjects. It was thus the idea of citizenship in its modern connotation which was conceived of by Mendelssohn and which he thought might benefit his Jewish brethren who lived under the jurisdiction of Frederick the Great. He developed this idea with convincing arguments, clothing it in language elegant, yet pithy and lucid. His conception amounted to what is nowadays known as separation of state and religion.

The argument running throughout Mendelssohn's dissertation is that religious faith should not constitute an impediment to the acquisition of citizenship. The final aims of both state and religion are similar, in that both strive for the welfare of the individual—the state for his physical well-being, and religion for his spiritual salvation. The state may enforce laws which appear objectionable to this or that individual citizen, provided that they were accepted by the majority of the people's elected representatives. The same applies to a monarch (like Fredrick the Great in Mendelssohn's time) who was considered as embodying the will of the people. The state is mainly interested in actions, though desirous of influencing the people's beliefs as well. Yet the citizen fulfills his civic duties if he complies with the laws enacted by the state, while in his heart he may either approve of or reject them. However, neither the church nor the state is empowered to force its views or beliefs on the citizen, and *a fortiori* the state cannot make certain privileges or rights dependent on the religious beliefs of the citizen. Mendelssohn bases himself on the theory of the social contract, which allegedly resulted from the willingness of the citizens to transfer their natural rights of self-defense—of both body and possessions—to the elected representatives of the community. He argues that the social contract was never meant to bestow on the state or the church the right to impose its views on the citizens, because by its very nature freedom of thought is not transferable.

Mendelssohn's ideas, as expressed in the first part of his *Jerusalem*, pertain, as we have seen, to the field of political philosophy. His main thesis in this part of the book is the separation of church and state, which he advocates in order to prepare the ground for the legal bestowal of equal rights on his Jewish co-religionists. This is the reason why he delineates the scope of jurisdiction of both state and church.

All the rights of the church amount to admonishing, teaching, supporting, and comforting. All that is required of the citizen in relation to the church is a willing ear and heart. The church has no right to reward or punish citizens for their actions. Civic actions pertain to the state. Purely religious conduct does not, by its very nature, tolerate compulsion or blandishments. It either emanates from the free inclination of the soul or it is an empty play, utterly alien to the true spirit of the religion.[1]

It is interesting to note that a Jew who had just emerged from the ghetto formulated the idea of separation of state and church with such remarkable zeal. No wonder that this aroused hostility and even the wrath of churchmen who saw in Mendelssohn's arguments a dangerous attempt to limit the authority and power of the church. Only protagonists of the philosophy of Enlightenment in the Christian world, notably Immanuel Kant, welcomed the appearance of Mendelssohn's *Jerusalem*, praising the acumen and subtlety it revealed.

Notwithstanding the fact that ostensibly neither the church nor the state has the right to impose beliefs and opinions, the rights of the state are in some ways more comprehensive and rigorous than those of the church. The state may indeed enforce actions in accordance with its laws, and mete out punishment for infringement of these laws. It may even in exceptional cases deprive subjects of their citizenship or even exile them; and all this under the social-contract theory. The church, on the other hand, can neither impose views or beliefs nor enforce religious conduct. The only weapon at its disposal is the exercise of influence and persuasion. Mendelssohn does not shrink back from pursuing this idea to its very end: the rejection of the right of excommunication and ostracism, which was practiced by Jewish communities against renegades and heretics throughout the Middle Ages and even in later centuries.

It might be recalled that Mendelssohn's *Jerusalem* was written in reply to those of his critics who argued that the idea of separation of state and religion in general, and the renunciation of ostracism of offenders against religious law, was contrary to the spirit of Judaism. Hence in the view of his opponents Mendelssohn had to choose between either remaining a Jew, loyal to his faith, or becoming an enlightened citizen of the German state. Mendelssohn's critics exemplified their objections in the following hypothetical case: Suppose that the Jewish community of Berlin employs an official whose duties include circumcision of newborn Jewish infants. The contract signed by both sides includes a statement of the official's duties, as well as the emoluments offered in return for his services. In the course of time this same official becomes beset by doubts as to the validity of this ancient rite, and so refuses to carry out the duties stipulated in the contract. Wouldn't the Jewish community cancel his contract and withdraw his emoluments and the other privileges connected with it? The foregoing example is, in the view of Mendelssohn's critics, typical of many possible situations of this kind.

Needless to say, it was easy for Mendelssohn to refute this accusation by simply pointing to the fact that the hypothetical official would not be punished for his change of heart and for holding certain opinions, but merely for breach of contract. If his conscience did not permit him to carry out the terms of his contract, then he must simply forgo the rights and benefits it bestows and cancel it.

We may gain an interesting insight into the religious problems caused by the profound changes in the social and civic status of the Jews in Mendelssohn's time if we consider and analyze another case reported in Mendelssohn's treatise, where a married Jewish woman applied for a divorce because her husband had converted to Christianity. Mendelssohn came across this case in an essay by a German writer called Friedrich Maurer entitled "The Search for Light and Right," published in Berlin in 1782. This same author supports the husband's refusal to grant his wife a divorce, arguing that in the name of freedom of thought the husband's change of religious convictions could not affect the marital contract. Mendelssohn, on the other hand, supported the wife's demand for divorce, claiming that she could not be compelled to acquiesce to a profound change in her way of life (brought about by her husband's conversion) which also affected the education of their children. In short, Mendelssohn maintains that the wife, too, was entitled to freedom of thought, and her husband's right to his convictions could not be bought at the expense of her own. The husband who brought about the change in their common way of life, which *mutatis mutandis* amounted to a breach in the conditions of the contract previously entered into, must bear the consequences and grant his wife the divorce desired by her.

However, there was one point of criticism launched against Mendelssohn at that time which he did not find so easy to refute, and which in his words "touched his heart." His critics claimed that there was a profound contradiction in his philosophical convictions. On the one hand he was the leading champion of separation of state and church, basing his demand for civic rights for the Jews on this very idea, and on the other hand he remained a Jew loyal to the laws and customs of Judaism, knowing full well that nonseparation of state and religion was inherent in it.

The right of the synagogue armed with sanctions against violation of religious law was always regarded as a cornerstone of the Jewish religion, forming one of the main articles in the doctrinal system of your fathers: How can you, my dear Mr. Mendelssohn, cleave to the faith of your fathers when you bring down

its whole structure by denying the synagogue's right of impos-
ing sanctions which was enjoined by Moses through divine
revelation?[2]

Mendelssohn admitted that this criticism cut him to the quick.
He must have been aware of the fact that during the first and
second Jewish commonwealths (and even later on, wherever Jews
enjoyed complete autonomy), religious law was regarded as the
only law applicable to members of the Jewish community and
therefore enforceable by means of sanctions.

> As far as offenses are concerned . . . Every transgression
> against the sovereignty of God, as Lawgiver of the nation, was
> an offense against His majesty and hence an offense against the
> state. He who vilifies God commits treason; he who desecrates
> the Sabbath violates a basic law of the state because upon the
> sanctity of His day rests a large part of the state constitution.[3]

In Mendelssohn's days the status of the Jews had undergone a
profound change, and Jewish laws were no longer enforceable;
their upholding depended entirely on the free consent of the
members of the community. Hence they were no longer subject to
a constitution of their own, but to the laws of the state authorities. Mendelssohn was aiming at a concept of citizenship which
was entirely divorced from religious allegiance, but based on
obedience to the laws of the state and readiness to fulfill civic
duties and obligations.

It goes without saying that Mendelssohn discerned clearly be-
hind all these criticisms the more or less articulate suggestion
that he forsake the faith of his fathers and adopt Christianity. He
countered this proposal with a theological argument, stressing
the fact that Christianity was based on Judaism and must of
necessity share its fate in many ways.

> Shall I, my dear one, take this step [of converting to Christian-
> ity] without first pondering whether it will really extricate me
> from the confusion in which you think I find myself. If it were
> true that the cornerstones of my house were so out of alignment

that the entire building threatened to collapse, would I be acting wisely if I attempted to save my belongings by moving them from the lower to the upper floor? Would I be safer there? Now Christianity, as you know, is built upon Judaism and must necessarily collapse along with it. When you say that my conclusions undermine the foundations of Judaism and you offer me the safety of your upper floor, must I not suspect that you mock me?[4]

As a loyal and proud Jew Mendelssohn was not prepared to pay the price of abandoning Judaism in return for the granting of civic rights for himself and his co-religionists. He states expressly that he would rather forgo the benefits of civic rights and maintain the inferior status quo of the Jews if civic equality was to be purchased by the exorbitant price of abandonment of Judaic law.[5]

That his conception of Judaism was strongly influenced by the rationalistic outlook of the Age of Enlightenment is by no means surprising. Equally understandable against the background of his time is his contention that religious faith does not constitute a phenomenon per se; but represents a kind of knowledge, which might be termed metaphysical, but which on last analysis is actually based on reason. This contention has far-reaching consequences. On the basis of the rationality of faith it may be argued, as Mendelssohn actually did, that there is no specific Judaic faith, but there are metaphysical verities based on reason which are therefore eternal and universal. Hence it is obvious that in Judaism there are not any commandments enjoining Jews to believe this or that religious verity, for Holy Scripture need not persuade us to accept what we recognize as valid by the natural light of reason. The divine commandments require action and conduct, and not religious faith.

Among all the commandments and injunctions of the Mosaic law there isn't a single one which says: "thou shalt believe" or "thou shalt not believe." But they all enjoin "thou shalt do" or "thou shalt not do." One can't command faith, because we do not accept any decrees other than such that are arrived at by way of conviction. All the divine behests are directed at man's will and power of action.[6]

Mendelssohn's conception of Judaism found its most pithy and lucid expression in the following passage in his *Jerusalem*.

To say it in one sentence: I believe that Judaism knows nothing of a revealed religion in the sense in which Christians understand this term. The Israelites possess a divine legislation—laws, commandments, ordinances, rules of life, instruction in the will of God, as to how they should conduct themselves in order to attain temporal and eternal felicity. What was revealed to them through Moses were rules and precepts of this kind, not doctrines, saving truths, or universally valid propositions of reason. These the Eternal One reveals to us and all other men at all times through the nature of things but not through the spoken or written word [of revelation].[7]

To put it briefly one might say that what Mendelssohn considers specific to Judaism is only Halakhah; all the rest is just natural religion, ultimately based on reason, and hence of a universal character. However, Halakhah naturally includes the so-called ceremonial law, i.e., the dietary laws, laws prohibiting the wearing of clothes containing a mixture of linen and wool, and many others whose rationality is by no means clear. It is not surprising that the enlightened philosopher Mendelssohn makes an original attempt to justify them rationally on the following grounds: The ceremonial law, just because of its lack of rational transparency, calls for oral interpretation and explanation, which is best done through interaction between teacher and pupil. In other words it stimulates and motivates discussion and exchange of views, which is a most desirable consequence. Moreover, action and conduct are transitory, whereas printed symbols, images, religious relics are durable and permanent, and may, by misunderstanding and wrong interpretation, become conducive to idolatry. Hence one of the main purposes of the ceremonial law is to create a barrier against idolatry. To sum up, the ceremonial law constitutes a barrier against idolatry; it fosters a close and intimate connection between teacher and pupil, between religious doctrine and life.

Professor Alexander Altmann has an interesting retort to Mendelssohn's conception of the ceremonial law. He observes that

Mendelssohn failed to explain why Providence had left the rest of mankind without comparable legislation that would act as a barrier against idolatry and as a link between religious doctrine and life. "The same moral consideration that caused Mendelssohn to deny the revealed character of eternal verities should have suggested the need for universal revealed legislation."[8]

One might reply to this criticism in the spirit of Mendelssohn that the Jewish people as the guardian of ethical monotheism required special safeguards against idolatry. Moreover there is a "universal revealed legislation" binding upon mankind in the form of the seven Noahide laws, which, similar to the Ten Commandments, represent the fundamental moral basis of any civilized society.

All that has been said so far about Mendelssohn's interpretation of the ceremonial law cannot blur the obvious fact that his theory appears somewhat contrived. On the other hand, the attempt—or for that matter any attempt—to interpret and justify the commandments of the Torah whose rationale is by no means obvious is in the mainstream of traditional Jewish philosophy; indeed, it is one of its pervasive themes.[9] The question may be asked whether Mendelssohn made any concessions to gentile susceptibilities when delineating the main features of Judaism. Did he attempt to "groom" Judaism, and through it the Jewish people, so as to make them more eligible for the acquisition of civic rights? In order to answer this question, let us examine the structure of Mendelssohn's treatise *Jerusalem.* We have seen that the first part expounds the political philosophy of the Age of Enlightenment. His demands in this part of the essay are generally directed toward his German compatriots, who are persuaded to accept the logical consequences to be drawn from this philosophy, i.e., the separation of church and state. Once this theory is accepted, there can be no obstacle to the granting of civic rights to the Jews. The second part of his essay represents an exposition of Judaism in the light of the spirit of his time. It aims in particular at propounding the religious ideas that Jews have in common with non-Jews, drawing at the same time the dividing line between them, and this, as we have seen, is the ceremonial law, which is binding only for Jews.

It must be admitted that here Mendelssohn went rather far, in that he suggested the existence of a comprehensive common basis for Judaism and Christianity and *ipso facto* any other monotheistic religion as well. He did so by claiming that the whole doctrinal basis of Judaism was not peculiar to it, but characteristic of what might be termed "natural" religion.

By rationalizing the concept of faith and making it entirely an offshoot of reason, he showed that he had absorbed, undiluted, the more extreme features of the philosophy of his time. We cannot entirely eliminate the suspicion that he did so in order to bring about a rapprochement between Judaism and the gentile world, and therefore it cannot be dismissed out of hand that his presentation of Judaism displayed a certain amount of bias.

This is not to say that Mendelssohn was the first pronounced rationalist in the field of Jewish philosophy. There are some antecedents to his attitude, first in the person of Sa'adia Gaon, who by his well-known distinction between "rational precepts" and "revealed laws"—when classifying the mitzvot—and by stressing the independence of the former from revelational sources, created a common moral basis for the Jewish and gentile world. If rational precepts, such as most of the commandments of a social character, nevertheless appear as revealed laws in the Bible, Sa'adia Gaon maintains that this is so because there are many necessary details expounded in it (such as expiation of guilt, retribution, punishment, etc.) which might not have been known merely by the natural light of reason. A pronounced rationalistic attitude emerges from the following passage in Sa'adia Gaon's *Book of Beliefs and Opinions*.

The basis of our belief in the mission of Moses is not solely in the miracles and marvels that he performed. The reason for our believing in him and in every other prophet is rather the fact that he first called upon us to do what is proper. When we have heard his appeal and we saw that it was proper, we demanded from him miracles in support of it.[10]

In Sa'adia's view the concept of faith (*emunah*) is also based on reason, just as later on in the view of Mendelssohn, as the following paragraph from *The Book of Beliefs and Opinions* indicates. In it Sa'adia attempts to give a definition of faith.

We say that it is a notion that arises in the soul in regard to the actual character of anything that is apprehended. When the cream of investigation emerges and is embraced and enfolded by the minds (*Sechel*) and through them acquired and digested by the souls, then the person becomes convinced of the truth of the notion he has thus acquired.[11]

Further corroboration of the point mentioned may be found in the philosophy of Maimonides. Its strong rationalistic elements are too well known to require detailed elaboration. In his view even the highest realizations of religious genius—pure spiritual contemplation and the attainment of the spirit of prophecy—can in principle be achieved not only by Jews but also by non-Jews, because both of these highest attributes are, in Maimonides' last analysis, fruits of human intellectual and spiritual endeavor as well as moral virtue, and these qualities pertain to mankind in general. A modern Israeli expounder of Maimonides' philosophy sees in him "the first thinker in the history of medieval Jewish philosophy who viewed prophecy as a universal human quality, the attainment of which is in principle possible for both Jews and non-Jews."[12]

Enough has been said to show that Mendelssohn's place is to be found in traditional Jewish rationalistic philosophy. Nevertheless he has been severely criticized by representatives of almost all trends of thought within Jewish philosophy.

I have dealt elsewhere in detail with Samson Raphael Hirsch's criticism of Mendelssohn,[13] which is of course characteristic of Orthodoxy, and therefore I may summarize it briefly. Hirsch found fault with Mendelssohn's main preoccupation with the prevailing philosophy of his time and deplores his neglect of specific Jewish thought, a charge which is only partially justified, because the theme of Mendelssohn's *Jerusalem* deals precisely with Jewish philosophy (not to mention the monumental work of Bible translation and commentary as well as other writings of a Jewish character). Hirsch's second point of criticism is that Mendelssohn developed Judaism not in an immanent spirit, but from without, i.e., from the viewpoint of general rationalist philosophy, a charge which was contradicted by the historian Ze'ev Ya'avetz, who claims precisely the opposite, namely that Mendelssohn developed Judaism from within, presenting it mainly as revealed law "without emasculating it by means of a poor catechism . . . for Judaism is not a religion of the synagogue, but a religion of life, a religion for the soul and for the home, for both the people and the individual."[14]

The last two points of Hirsch's criticism—the charge that Mendelssohn neglected the Talmud, and that he displayed a strong desire to excel as a German philosopher while remaining a practicing Jew—seem more justified than those previously mentioned. If we now turn to criticisms of Mendelssohn's conception of Judaism which originated in circles not identified with traditional Judaism, we might mention the objections raised by Zionist thinkers, such as the modern Hebrew writer Peretz Smolenskin, who found fault with Mendelssohn's attempt to reduce Judaism to its minimal dimensions, namely the set of *mitzvot ma'asiot,* and deplored the "contraction" (*tzimtzum*) of Judaism at the hands of Mendelssohn. More surprising is the criticism which emanated from the liberal Jewish circles to which the medical doctor and philosopher Solomon Ludwig Steinheim belonged. The latter, in his work *Moses Mendelssohn und seine Schule* (published 1840), castigates him, not unlike Smolenskin, for having emptied Judaism of its doctrinal content and specific faith. He goes so far as to call Mendelssohn a gentile as far as his mind is concerned, and a Jew in the physical sense—inasmuch as he was capable of performing the mitzvot which are enjoined by God.

It should be borne in mind that most of these criticisms were voiced in retrospect after it had become clear in which direction German Jewry was headed after the Emancipation. Needless to say, some of the blame for the wave of assimilation and even apostasy in the aftermath of its Emancipation was put on Mendelssohn's shoulders. A fairer and more reasoned judgment of this turn of events will point to the sudden and revolutionary change in the life and status of the Jews which was brought about by the Emancipation. This sudden and precipitous upheaval—in the gentile world the transition from medieval to modern times lasted for centuries—made a more balanced adjustment of Jewish life to the newly created circumstances extremely difficult. And so it appears to me idle to speculate to what extent Mendelssohn's conception of Judaism contributed to the acceleration of the process of assimilation of European Jewry. In any case it would be unfair to isolate one particular treatise from a whole conglomerate of historical forces active at that time and make it responsible for so profound a change in the religious life of the Jewish people. Judged per se, i.e., as a philosophy of Judaism, Mendelssohn's *Jerusalem* is in line with the mainstream of rationalism in traditional Jewish thought and does not represent a fundamental deviation from its true spirit.

To conclude, I wish to quote Heinrich Heine's remarks about Mendelssohn's *Jerusalem*.

> Though rejecting tradition, he sought to uphold the Mosaic ceremonial law as religiously binding. Was it out of cowardice or wisdom? Was it a melancholy and nostalgic love which deterred him from laying destructive hands on matters which in his ancestors' views were of the holiest, and for which so much blood and tears of martyrdom were shed? I do not think so. Just as kings of worldly affairs, so have kings of the spirit to be unassailable by feelings of family attachment. Even on the heights of enthroned thought one must not indulge in ease and comfort.[15]

This eloquent tribute paid to Mendelssohn may sound somewhat exaggerated, though allowance has to be made for the fact that its author was a poet. However it contains a point which should be disputed. Mendelssohn did not reject the Jewish tradition and he himself would have protested violently against any such allegation; as has already been pointed out, he tried to adapt Jewish tradition to newly emerging circumstances while doing all in his power to preserve its most essential features.

Finally, rejecting tradition is not concomitant with seeking to preserve the "Mosaic ceremonial law as religious obligation," unless Heine meant by Jewish tradition, the style and external appurtenances of ghetto life, a poetic license which may be granted to him.

2

Samson Raphael Hirsch and *Torah im Derekh Erez*

Though famous, Samson Raphael Hirsch is now but little read. His personality and work are sufficiently known in Israel. In the Diaspora, the publication in London of an English edition of some of his writings[1] and the splendid edition of the Hirsch Chumash in English (translated by Hirsch's grandson, Dr. Isaac Levy, and containing a massive introduction by Rabbi I. Grunfeld) are likely to mark a turning point in English Jewry's interest in S. R. Hirsch. It is to be expected that this magnum opus of Hirsch will exercise an influence on the Jewish religious scene in all English-speaking countries.

In Israel the situation is different. There his influence, slight as it is, is actually on the decline, and this in spite of the fact that a fair proportion of his writings have been translated into Hebrew. True, he is appreciated for his devotion to the cause of traditional Judaism and for having propounded a philosophic basis for Orthodoxy; true, he is mentioned in textbooks of Jewish history used in all Israeli schools, and a number of his articles in Hebrew translation are included in anthologies of Jewish thought used in religious high schools and secondary yeshivot in Israel. Nevertheless, ultra-Orthodox circles tend to ignore Hirsch's conception of Judaism, and, in their spiritual isolation, look askance at the work of a thinker whose writings display a marked "extrovert" tendency—a tendency which to them appears suspect.

There are three reasons for the lack of interest in Hirsch's writings. First, his involved and flowery style is a hindrance to easy reading. Secondly, one who reads his work in German, or, for that matter, in English or Hebrew translation, cannot fail to be aware how much his ideas, though fundamentally Jewish, were steeped in contemporary German thought. No wonder that some Jewish historians, notably Wiener and Elbogen, considered him a typical nineteenth-century German-Jewish intellectual, not altogether unlike his most outspoken liberal opponents. It is no easy task to extract the pure Jewish content of his thinking from the trappings and intricate convolutions of mid-nineteenth-century German thought in which it is wrapped.

The third reason lies in Hirsch's apparent lack of nationalistic feeling. He believed in the universal mission of the religion of Israel and in its fulfillment through the dispersal of the people of Israel. He believed that the Jewish people, by living an exemplary life, could bring the nations of the world to realize the truth of the Jewish faith and long to attain it. This belief in the universal mission of the Jewish people in the Diaspora and in the passive hope of bringing the Redeemer through righteous conduct (rather than by active participation in the attainments of political independence of the nation) is expressed in the sixteenth of his *Nineteen Letters*.[2] There he says:

Land and soil were never Israel's bond of union, but only the common task of the Torah; therefore [Israel] still forms a united body, though separated from a national soil; nor does this unity lose its reality, though Israel accepts everywhere the citizenship of the nations among which it is dispersed. This coherence of sympathy, this spiritual union, which may be designated by the Hebrew terms *am* and *goy*, but not by the expression "nation," unless we are able to separate from the term the concept of common territory and political power, is the only communal bond we possess, or ever expect to possess, until the great day shall arrive when the Almighty shall see fit, in His inscrutable wisdom, to unite again His scattered servants in one land, and

the Torah shall be the guiding principle of a state, an exemplar
of the meaning of Divine Revelation and the mission of humanity.

For this future, which is promised us in the glorious predictions of the inspired prophets, whom God raised up for our
ancestors, we hope and pray; but actively to accelerate its
coming is a sin, and is prohibited to us, while the entire
purpose of the Messianic age is that we may, in prosperity,
exhibit to mankind a better example of "Israel" than did our
ancestors the first time, while, hand in hand with us, mankind
will be joined in universal brotherhood through the recognition
of God, the All-One.

Undoubtedly Hirsch cannot be numbered among the suppor-
ters of the national ideal in its politico-secular meaning, or among
the Chovevei Zion, whose ideas were nurtured in the spiritual
climate of Eastern European Jewry. His idealism was a religious
and not a nationalistic one. Hirsch exalted the Jewish faith above
other faiths, thought of it as the "religion of religions," and, like
the author of the *Kuzari,* considered the people of Israel as
endowed with a religious capacity fundamentally different from
that of other peoples. This point is clearly brought out in Rabbi Y.
Y. Weinberg's article on Hirsch, in which he says: "Rabbi Hirsch,
whose essential thought was to regard the Jewish people as the
axis around which all world history revolves, must be deemed as
an extreme nationalist in heart and spirit, a religio-ethical rather
than a secular nationalist."[3]

Hirsch's thought has many facets, reflected in a literary produc-
tion that is vast and many-sided. He excelled as an original
commentator on the Pentateuch, the Psalms, and the prayer
book. He added greatly to our understanding of the meaning of
the biblical commandments. His observations on symbolism in
Judaism are embodied in two substantial essays as well as in his
commentary to the Pentateuch (but have not yet received their
rightful evaluation and appreciation). Moreover, he was also a
man of action, and while he was rabbi of Nikolsburg, Moravia,
from 1848 to 1851, he helped to further the cause of equality of
rights for the Jews. He worked for the unification of the Jewish

communities of Moravia and the creation of a single organization to which they were all to belong. Later, when he was rabbi in Frankfurt, he fought successfully for an independent organization of the Orthodox Jewish communities in Germany. But his greatest contribution was in the field of education. He was a noted educational philosopher as well as a practicing pedagogue, acting as headmaster of what was then a unique school. It was there that his influence was most felt, and that influence has, to some extent, continued until the present.

The greatest problem he had to face was how to integrate Jewish and European culture, how to effect a relationship between sacred and secular studies in the school. This problem can be seen clearly only when the historical position of post-Emancipation European Jewry is known.

The Emancipation came suddenly and found Jewry unprepared. Whereas in Christian society the process of secularization had been a long one, and the change from a religious to a secular culture had taken hundreds of years, the Jews had to adapt themselves to the change in a very few years. When the gates of the ghetto were opened, they found it difficult to accustom themselves to the freethinking cultural and social life of the countries in which they lived. They failed to grasp the character of such a culture, for it was alien to them, and acclimatization to the new way of life was an arduous process. How was the continued existence of Judaism to be ensured in this new environment? The greatest stumbling block to integration with the strange community was the Jewish religion itself, which "ordained a different speech, a different dress, different food, different ways of rejoicing and mourning, and different mode of thought. The Jew was far more Jewish than the Christian was Christian."[4]

Judaism as practiced in the ghettos was no longer viable, and so there arose the question of how to adapt it, if it was to continue to exist at all, to the changed conditions. Reform circles tried to establish what they thought to be the essence of Judaism, and chose the historical method as a means of distinguishing between what they called the "spiritual content" of Judaism and what had been grafted on Judaism by accident of historical circumstance. They regarded as a disturbing element not only the dress and language of the Jews but also those positive statutes which became difficult of fulfillment in an alien environment and whose very right to existence seemed to them dubious. From such sources sprang their opposition to Jewish laws dealing with man's relationship to God, and their antagonism to the Talmud and the rabbinic interpretation of Judaism.

Hirsch chose a completely different solution. Like Rabbi Yehuda Halevi, he accepted the Torah as a fact as "real as heaven and earth," a creation analogous to nature itself. This analogy of Torah and nature he developed in the eighteenth of his *Letters*.

A word here concerning the true method of Torah-investigation. Two revelations are open before us, nature—and Torah. In nature all phenomena stand before us as indisputable facts, and we can only endeavor *a posteriori* to ascertain the law of each and the connection of all. Abstract demonstration of the truth or, rather, the probability of theoretic explanations of the facts of nature, is an unnatural proceeding. The right method is to verify our assumptions by the known facts, and the highest attainable degree of certainty is to say, "The facts agree with our assumption"—that is, all observed phenomena can be explained according to our theory. A single contradictory phenomenon will make our theory untenable. We must, therefore, acquire all possible knowledge concerning the object of our investigation, and know it, if possible, in its totality. If, however, all efforts should fail in disclosing the inner law and connection of phenomena revealed to us as facts in nature, the facts remain, nevertheless, undeniable, and cannot be reasoned away. The same principles must be applied to the investigation of the Torah. In the Torah, as in nature, God is the ultimate cause; in the Torah, as in nature, no fact may be denied, even though the reason and the connection may not be comprehended; as in nature, so in the Torah, the traces of Divine wisdom must ever be sought for. Its ordinances must be accepted in their entirety as undeniable phenomena, and must be studied in accordance with their connection with each other and the subject to which they relate. Our conjectures must be tested by their precepts, and our highest certainty here also can only be that everything stands in harmony with our theory. But, as in nature, the phenomena are recognized as facts, though their cause and relation to each other may not be understood, and are independent of our investigation . . . in the same way the ordinances of the Torah must be law for us, even if we do not comprehend the reason and the purpose of a single one. Our fulfillment of the commandments must not depend upon our investigations.

To this analogy of nature and Torah must be added a second point essential to our understanding of the fundamentals of Hirsch's outlook—the relationship between Judaism and history. We have mentioned that the Reformists of his time, such as Geiger, Frankel, and Holdheim, used the historical criterion as a means of adapting the Jewish faith to the post-Emancipation conditions of life. Hirsch opposed this historical approach to Judaism because he rejected the view that Judaism was subject to the historical process. Nathan Rotenstreich explains this position in the following way:

Hirsch thought it possible to save the [Judaic] legal order, which is innately static and not easily altered from the corrosive action of the historical process. The legal sphere is one where permanent features are more prominent than transient ones, where the enduring has sway over the mutable. The preference for law over doctrine and faith reflects a certain conception of the essence of Judaism. . . . Preference for Jewish law reflects a tendency to withdraw the true essence of Judaism from the historical process, posing it incontrovertibly as divinely revealed and an eternal statute.[5]

In his critical survey of Samson Raphael Hirsch's *Nineteen Letters*, Geiger vehemently rejects the analogy of Torah and nature. "Hirsch surely cannot seriously believe," writes Geiger,

that his apodictic statement that Torah is as factually real as heaven and earth expresses an alternative theory to the historical proof. In this way, all religions could attribute absolute authority to the books on which they base their ideas, such as the Koran and the Gospels. How can one compare Torah to nature when the latter is a lofty and incomprehensible creation which cannot be examined exhaustively, whose beginning and end are difficult to grasp, and which stands above the power of man? On the other hand, Torah is a book intended solely for us and is subject to the historical process; its age can be estimated accurately.

Geiger concludes this paragraph of criticism with the words: "For goodness sake, what an error have we here! May God save Israel from such a spirit!"[6]

Geiger's criticism of Hirsch seems pertinent enough at first sight, and Hirsch's assumption of the analogous character of Torah and nature indeed sounds dogmatic, unless we modify Hirsch's analogy and say that in some ways Torah may be equated with natural law, an idea that has its antecedents in the history of Jewish thought and was adopted by Hirsch's grandson Isaac Breuer.

In view of such a profound difference of opinion over so basic a matter, any further discussion between Hirsch and Geiger would have been fruitless and a compromise between the two views unlikely. In Hirsch's opinion, it was impossible to adjust Judaism to the spirit of the times; he believed that the Torah was a criterion by which we should assess the ideas of the times and reject that which failed to measure up to the Torah's lofty divine spirit.

In order to develop more clearly his religious attitude and give it a firm theological basis, Hirsch considered it necessary to evaluate critically Mendelssohn's philosophy of Judaism. This was essential, since Mendelssohn's philosophy, accepted by many Western European Jews, appeared dangerous to Hirsch, and this danger became greater as Mendelssohn's ideas passed to his pupils and to those who continued his work. Hirsch's criticism of Mendelssohn was expressed in the eighteenth of his *Letters* in these words:

This commanding individual, who had not drawn his mental development from Judaism, who was great chiefly in philosophical disciplines, in metaphysics, and aesthetics, who treated the Bible only philologically and aesthetically, and did not build up Judaism as a science from itself, but merely defended it against political stupidity and pietistic Christian audacity, and who was personally an observant Jew, accomplished this much, that he showed the world and his brethren that it was possible to be a strictly religious Jew and yet to shine distinguished as the German Plato.

This "and yet" was decisive. His followers contented themselves with developing Bible study in the philologic-aesthetic sense, with studying the Moreh, and with pursuing and spreading humanistic letters; but Judaism, Bible and Talmud, as Jewish science, were neglected. Even the most zealous study of the Bible was of no avail for the comprehension of Judaism, because it was not treated as the authoritative source of doctrine and instruction, but only as a beautiful poetic storehouse from which to draw rich supplies for the fancy and the imagination. The Talmud thus neglected, practical Judaism thus completely uncomprehended, it was but natural that the former symbolizing and abstract interpretation of Judaism, which had for a time been interrupted, again became prevalent and was carried to an extreme which threatened to destroy all Judaism.[7]

Four things, then, are clear: (1) Hirsch found fault with Mendelssohn's main preoccupation with the general philosophies and his neglect of specific Jewish thought; (2) according to Hirsch, Mendelssohn developed Judaism not in an immanent spirit but from without—that is, from the viewpoint of the general rationalist philosophies; (3) what really angered Hirsch was Mendelssohn's excessive desire to excel as an eminent German philosopher while remaining a practicing Jew; (4) the Talmud was neglected by Mendelssohn, and his followers no longer saw in it an authoritative source of Jewish doctrine.

Mendelssohn was one of the last philosophers to believe that it was possible to prove theological and metaphysical truths as rationally as mathematical ones. Mendelssohn admitted that metaphysical truth is more complicated and harder to grasp than the laws and theorems of mathematics, but he believed that metaphysical truth is equally universal and immutable. Mendelssohn, therefore, denied that there is a specific faith for the Jewish people, confirmed, as it were, by divine revelation, because faith, according to Mendelssohn, is based on reason, and reason is universal and common to all men. Hirsch's criticism of Mendelssohn for considering Judaism not from a Jewish but from a universal standpoint is, I think, understandable and justified.

Whereas Mendelssohn preserved, as a historical legacy of Sinai, the validity of the practical commandments, which he regarded as the essence of Judaism, we cannot deny that by his insistence on the commandments alone, and by his neglect of the peculiar faith that inspired them, he narrowed the concept of Judaism. This caused a dichotomy in his Jewish outlook, a split which became a danger for those who followed him. He was a Jew in that he complied with the commandments of the Torah, but as a philosopher he belonged to the thinkers of the Enlightenment (Haskalah).

When speaking of Hirsch's attitude to the relationship of the Torah to universal culture and of the contradictions that such a comparison reveals, mention must be made of Hirsch's biting criticism of Maimonides' attitude to this same problem as expressed in Letter Eighteen.

This great man, to whom, and to whom alone, we owe the preservation of practical Judaism to our time, is responsible because he sought to reconcile Judaism with the difficulties which confronted it from without, instead of developing it creatively from within, for all the good and the evil which bless and afflict the heritage of the fathers. His peculiar mental tendency was Arabic-Greek, and his conception of the purpose of life the same. He entered into Judaism from without, bringing with him opinions of whose truth he had convinced himself from extraneous sources and—he reconciled. For him, too, self-perfecting through the knowledge of truth was the highest aim, the practical he deemed subordinate. For him knowledge of God was the end, not the means; hence he devoted his intellectual powers to speculations upon the essence of Deity, and sought to bind Judaism to the results of his speculative investigations as to postulates of science or faith. The Mitzvoth became for him merely ladders, necessary only to conduct to knowledge or to protect against error, this latter often only the temporary and limited error of polytheism. Mishpatim became only rules of prudence, Mitzvoth as well; Chukkim rules of health, teaching right feeling, defending against the transitory errors of the time; Edoth ordinances, designed to promote philosophical or other concepts; all this having no foundation in the eternal essence of things, not resulting from their eternal demand on me, or from my eternal purpose and task, no eternal symbolizing of an unchangeable idea, and not inclusive enough to form a basis for the totality of the commandments.[8]

Two points in this criticism of Maimonides' *Guide* need special attention. The first is the argument that Maimonides in the *Guide* did not creatively develop Judaism from its intrinsic qualities but rather entered it from without and imposed upon it alien attitudes—in this case, the Aristotelian ideal of a contemplative life and the perfection of man through meditation upon the concept of an abstract Godhead. The second point springs from the first: if the contemplative life expresses the highest value, it is clear that the positive, practical side of Judaism—that is, fulfilling the commandments—is of secondary and subordinate importance. In other words, in Hirsch's opinion, there appears in the *Guide to the Perplexed* a kind of relativization of the commandments, whereas in Hirsch's view they have a supreme value and validity which is eternal. This is the source of Hirsch's constant demand for developing Judaism immanently, from within itself (*sich selbst begreifendes Judentum*).

Hirsch, himself an admirer of the secular intellectual environment of his time, did not object to Maimonides' and Mendelssohn's interest in non-Jewish philosophies but to the way they used them. Synthesis cannot be imposed from without, but like a flower opening to the sun, can only be reached from within.

But was Orthodox European Jewry ready, in the middle of the nineteenth century, to consider the possibility of a synthesis of any kind?

Heinemann, in his introduction to the *Nineteen Letters*, sums up the antagonistic attitudes of traditional Jewry to European culture with the pithy and pointed talmudic proverb, "I want neither your sting nor your honey." This saying epitomizes the rabbinical viewpoint from the Middle Ages down to the time of S. R. Hirsch. The following are two typical facts that exemplify this approach: (1) In the last years of Rabbi Pinhas Hurwitz, author of *Hafla'ah* (died 1805), a group of *Maskilim* in Frankfurt began to draw up a scheme for a school of secular studies which would complement the traditional education provided at cheder and Talmud Torah. The children would have lessons in German, arithmetic, and French; in all, two or three hours a day. Hurwitz and his followers were bitterly opposed to this scheme, and to prevent its realization placed a ban (excommunication) on the school. The local authorities intervened on behalf of the school and declared the ban of excommunication illegal, hoping thereby to force Rabbi Hurwitz into annulling it. The rabbi fought against this decision, and not only did he refuse to submit but complained to higher authorities about the interference of the Frankfurt Senate in internal Jewish affairs.[9] (2) Abraham Geiger relates an interesting episode from his childhood. On his becoming Bar Mitzvah in 1823, he delivered a discourse of a general ethical nature. The speech was delivered in German, but he had to preface his address with an introduction in Judeo-German, and when he began to speak pure German many of the people present covered their faces in shame.[10]

This was the trend when Hirsch began his activities as a rabbi and writer. However, during the following decades the process of assimilation among German Jewry developed rapidly until, by 1851, when Hirsch came to Frankfurt, only a small remnant of the old Orthodoxy still existed. Nonetheless, Hirsch, in spite of his zeal for European culture and his hope of attaining a synthesis of Jewish and European education in the spirit of *Torah im derekh erez*, did not regard this ideal as a concession to the new liberalism. He advanced his ideas as an integral part of his general outlook on Judaism. His views on this point may be summarized as follows: Unlike other religions, Judaism does not only aim at raising man's spirit and directing it toward God at certain times and on set occasions. Judaism is a way of life that permeates every aspect of a man's life, deeds, and thought. In the new reality of the post-Emancipation era Jews could isolate or dissociate themselves from the prevailing intellectual climate but had nevertheless to recognize the new spiritual environment and evaluate it by the standards of the Torah. To make this evaluation demanded a profound understanding of intellectual trends in the world around them.

It is for this reason that Hirsch insisted that Jews take part in the intellectual life of the gentiles and assess every attainment by the eternal criterion of the Torah. Moreover, divinity is revealed not only in the Torah but also in nature and in history. It therefore becomes essential to study nature and, through nature, learn to worship God, since "the heavens declare the glory of God and the firmament showeth His handiwork." The influence of God in the historical process is manifested in Divine Providence revealed both in the phenomena of nature and in the history of mankind. Divinity reveals itself, too, in the spirit of man, in great works of art and literature, and in every creative activity of man. This idea lies at the root of Hirsch's *Torah im derekh ereẓ* conception. Hence his reverence for cultural phenomena, his readiness to study the arts and sciences, and to be impressed by them. Thus Hirsch introduced a fresh note into the Ashkenazi (German-Jewish) intellectual climate of his time.

Still, we must admit that Hirsch occasionally weakened his position by explaining, as he did, that his principle of *Torah im derekh ereẓ* requires the sciences to be taught at school only as aids to a clearer understanding of the Torah and Halakhah (*Hilfswissenschaft*). For example, in his commentary on the verse in chapter 18 of Leviticus ("Mine ordinances shall ye do, and My statutes shall ye keep, to walk therein, I am the Lord your God"), Hirsch, citing *Torat Kohanim,* states that the seemingly superfluous words "to walk therein" point to a special emphasis.

> "To walk therein": to make them the main aim and not the subordinate one; to absorb oneself wholly in them and not mix other things with them; that you do not say, "I have learned the wisdom of Israel, now I shall learn the wisdom of the world." Therefore, it says "to walk therein"—you are not permitted to release yourself from them at all.

It seems as if this statement completely negates the study of the sciences, and if so, it would refute Hirsch's attitude. But his ingenious exegesis to eliminate the apparent contradiction itself emphasizes Hirsch's perspective: if it says "that to do them is the main and not the subordinate aim," it follows that it was not the studying of foreign wisdom that was forbidden but absorbing oneself in it to the exclusion of all else. Thus, Hirsch finds a logical basis for regarding sciences as subsidiary—that is, as an aid to a profounder understanding of the Torah.

This passage represents a rather narrow conception of the relationship between Torah and world culture—a conception that hardly appears representative of the man when we study the rest of his writings on this subject. Looking at his work as a whole, one can hardly doubt that it reflects a new emphasis on general culture as a vital complement to Judaism. His articles on this subject reveal an enthusiasm for Western literature and culture that is not to be found in other traditional Jewish thinkers. Many examples of this enthusiasm can be found in his writings. One especially impressive one is his speech given at the Hirsch School on the occasion of the fiftieth anniversary of Schiller's birth.

Schiller's poetry, said Hirsch, is permeated with true idealism. His belief in liberty, fraternity, and the rule of justice springs from a definitely religious outlook. Hirsch wondered greatly at this, and blessed Schiller with the traditional formula, "Blessed be He who allows other men to partake of His wisdom." He saw an echo of the Hebrew prophets in Schiller's poetic works and rejoiced at this. It is very possible that his optimistic attitude toward contemporary German idealism sprang from his appreciation of the post-Emancipation era, which he regarded as the "beginning of redemption" not only for Israel but also for all the people of the world.

Hirsch' disciples have subdivided the concept of *Torah im derekh erez* used by him into four categories.

1. The arts or sciences may be studied as the basis for a person's livelihood. This idea is to a large extent acceptable in traditional Judaism, not only as legitimate but as laudable and necessary. When the rabbis in the *Ethics of the Fathers* state, "An excellent thing is the study of Torah combined with some worldly occupation, for the labor demanded by them both makes sin to be

forgotten," the term "worldly occupation" does not only imply handicrafts, manual work, or trade, but also the professional occupations based on the study of the arts and sciences—the so-called free professions.

2. The arts and sciences may also serve as auxiliaries to Torah study. The natural and social sciences impinge upon many problems dealt with by Halakhah, in a wider sense help in the understanding of Judaism and its application to everyday life. In other words, *derekh erez* here is entirely in the service of Torah study and enhances its proper understanding and interpretation. It is the servant of Torah.

3. The study of the arts and sciences is a means of understanding man's inner world as well as his surrounding outer one. Man's outlook on life is to a large extent influenced by knowledge derived from the arts and sciences. The modern Jew must be able to relate this to the knowledge derived from the sources of traditional Judaism. This may of course give rise to conflicts which require carefully worked out solutions.

4. This category is connected with the previous one, spelling out, as it does, the rabbinical dictum "know what to answer the unbeliever." Accepting this idea in its wider sense, Hirsch saw it as involving a deep understanding of the surrounding cultures and their beliefs which enables the Jew to weigh and compare, and if necessary to defend, the tenets of Judaism.

Other interpreters of Hirsch look upon him as a thinker whose main achievement was the rehabilitation of ancient Judaism rather than a novel and revolutionary interpretation of it. It all depends on whether he is viewed against the background of medieval or premedieval Judaism. Rabbi Grunfeld says on this point:

If anything had been forced on the Jew, it was not his adherence to, but his exclusion from, general culture and education. When at the beginning of the nineteenth century the Jews again found their way into the world of science and general education they came in reality back to their own. For the estrangement was not organic but superimposed. It had by no means arisen from the essential character of Judaism. Just the contrary was true, as the golden eras of Jewish history in Babylonia and Spain had shown. In those eras the highest Talmudic and general scientific efficiency were combined. Apart from the enormous support which the study of Torah, Mishnah, and Talmud receives from secular knowledge, the whole task of the Jew as a servant of God in this world depends on his insight into the natural historical and social conditions around him.[11]

This same point is made by Rabbi Weinberg in the article mentioned previously. In his opinion, at the time of the tannaim, the amoraim, the geonim of Babylon, and the Golden Age of Spain, Judaism embraced every facet of intellectual and spiritual life. The change came at the time of the Crusades. Only as a result of persecution, atrocities, and the restriction of liberty of movement did there appear spiritual isolation and segregation. Thus Rabbi Weinberg, too, does not regard Hirsch as a revolutionary innovator, but as one who continued the tradition of premedieval Judaism.

The Orthodox post-Hirschian philosophers of the German school—Isaac Breuer, Yeshayahu Leibowitz—easily identifiable by their Neo-Orthodox proclivities, have accepted Hirsch's peculiar attitude to the law as "Judaism's innermost substance and core" (Wiener). More important still, they share Hirsch's breadth of mind, his refusal to view Judaism as rigorously self-contained, his belief in its universal aspects, its humanistic message, and its willingness to enter into partnership with general culture, welcoming the achievements of the human spirit, whatever their source, as long as they do not contradict fundamental tenets of Judaism.

3

Jewish Philosophy in Transition to an Ideology: Critique of Isaac Breuer's Philosophy of Judaism

Among English-speaking Jewry, Isaac Breuer is mainly known as a political leader who was active in German-Jewish politics during the first decades of this century. He is widely recognized and acknowledged as one of the most prominent founders of Agudat Israel (later, after his immigration to what was then Palestine, of its Labor wing—Poalei Agudat Israel) and as a highly articulate protagonist of independent Orthodoxy in Jewish communal life and organization.

However, Breuer was also a prolific writer in the field of Jewish philosophy. His literary work, in the form of treatises, philosophic novels and novelettes, pamphlets and articles published in Germany—a small part of which has appeared in Hebrew and English translation[1]—runs into thousands of pages. His political and philosophical writings are closely interwoven, his Jewish philosophy forming the basis from which spring his ideological and political stances. His Jewish religious thought might therefore be characterized as primarily active, for its basic tenets rarely remain exclusively in the sphere of theory, but spill over into the realm of Jewish life and political organization.

The present chapter aims mainly at a critical exposition of

31

Breuer's philosophical thought. Assuming that any system of thought is subject to historical development, though as far as Jewish traditional thought is concerned, its static elements by far outweigh those in flux and capable of development—assuming this to be true, a number of questions suggest themselves: What has this highly gifted and erudite man contributed to Jewish philosophy? Are there any novel features noticeable in his thought? Has his thought proved to be seminal in any way? Has he asked questions and suggested answers that were not thought of before? Does his traditionalism bear the imprint of the influence of contemporary philosophical thought, not exclusively Jewish? Is his mode of argument congenial and hospitable to the intellectual qualities as well as the idiosyncrasies of modern man?

Breuer's philosophical thought is not concerned with any side issues of Jewish philosophy, but with its basic and central themes. In his *Der Neue Kusari*, published in 1934—an ambitious work, as its title already indicates, and the most complete and masterly summary of his philosophical thought—he is engaged in a serious attempt to show the Jewish skeptic a way leading to Judaism. It is only natural that for Breuer this means a way to Jewish Orthodoxy of the independent stream. In other words, he is trying to build up a case for *Torah min ha-Shamayim* in its traditional sense, but of his own particular brand. He may thus be justly characterized as Orthodox, though his particular kind of Orthodoxy is permeated by a considerable measure of sophistication. Having assumed the role of a guide to the perplexed of our time, he is naturally compelled to confront all the main ideologies that loomed large in the intellectual climate of the first decades of this century, such as capitalism, Marxism, Zionism both secular and religious, and Jewish heterodoxy—especially German-Jewish Liberalism and Reform. In short, he does not leave aside any of the issues that challenged Orthodox Judaism, assuming the mantle of a latter-day defender of the Jewish traditional faith.

It may be opportune to start with a rather ambitious idea of Breuer's—at least to me it so appears—a thesis concerning the divine origin and literary inspiration of the Torah. As a matter of fact, Breuer's claim is even more far-reaching than that, for he endeavors literally to present "proofs" (to be precise one direct and one indirect) of the divine character of Holy Writ. I will now attempt to offer an exposition of both.

Breuer's indirect proof is associated with what may be called the unredeemed state of mankind: its perpetual wars, sufferings, and tribulations; in Breuer's own words, "the anarchy of the history of the nations."[2] This is exemplified in our time by such events as the wars in Indochina (Vietnam, Cambodia, etc.) with their horrific aftermath, the invasion of Afghanistan, the Iraq-Iran war, and the phenomenon of international terrorism.

The following is a more extensive quotation in English translation of the point made by Breuer.

> Perceptive intellects amongst the nations have always recognized this anarchy in the affairs of mankind, and have reacted to it with the deepest pain and sorrow. They have refused to find consolation in the achievements of civilization, in art or religion. Others have taken refuge in Utopias, or alternatively, they have combated force with force. To no avail. The whole of mankind lives, as it were, in Galut.[3]

Breuer's idea requires further elucidation. It has to be borne in mind that for Breuer—himself a lawyer—the legal aspect of the Torah is of crucial importance. Just as the Jewish Galut is regarded by the Hebrew prophets as a punishment for the breach of the Covenant, so is the suffering of mankind—metaphorically speaking, its Galut—the result of the breach of those fundamental moral precepts which are of a universal character, and therefore binding on the whole of mankind. Hence both the Galut of the Jews as well as that of the gentiles indirectly bear out the divine predictions of the Torah and the prophets.

As for the direct proof, this is to be perceived not only in the survival of the Jewish people in spite of its incredible sufferings and tribulations—a point already made by other thinkers—but mainly in the content of the admonitions specified in Leviticus chapter 25, and Deuteronomy chapter 28, in particular by the prediction of Israel's loss of statehood and exile.

In Breuer's own words:

There is no precedent in all the history of mankind for a proud and free people, which is attached to its soil as no other, and for whose statehood it would shed its last drops of blood, that such a nation should guard as a holy document the prediction of its own dispersal. There is no precedent in all the history of mankind for such a prediction to become literally fulfilled. It is amazing that a proud, free nation should bear witness to its own dispersal and suffer martyrdom at the hands of nations filled with hostility and hate toward it.[4]

Three points stand out clearly in Breuer's argument: First, the prophetic prediction of a nation's doom whilst it still lives freely and securely on its own soil. Second, that such a prediction should be enshrined in this nation's holiest book, and third, that this prediction should be so overwhelmingly borne out by historical events, and shape the destiny of the Jewish people throughout the ages.

In a later work Breuer enumerates in great detail the various features of the Jewish destiny which bear out the truth of the divine predictions.[5] The following are the manifestations called by Breuer *Gottestaten*—"acts of God": the Jewish homeland remains barren, waiting for the return of the Jewish people; the wanderings of the Diaspora Jews, of whole communities; the uprooted nation remains faithful to its land; what were formerly the laws of the state are preserved in the memory of the people as binding injunctions; wherever the wandering nation sets foot it is met with hostility; anguish is felt by the exiled Jews both in the ghettos of the Middle Ages and even in the midst of the process of assimilation in modern times; the exiled Jews preserve their national identity and uphold the covenant with God, expressed in the observance of the divine laws and commandments; the ineradicable Jewish awareness that the Diaspora represents atonement for the nation's transgressions and failings.

For all these reasons Breuer speaks of the "metahistorical" nature of Jewish history, meaning by this that the course of Jewish history is more pronouncedly permeated by Divine Providence than the history of the gentiles. He maintains this distinction despite his awareness that a more scientifically orientated historiography would by no means accept a viewpoint so manifestly tinged by theology. He even goes so far as to view Jewish history as a series of *Geschichtswunder*, meaning by this that it reveals a succession of events of a miraculous nature, termed by him "metahistorical," and distinct from the miracles which in the account of the Scriptures have occurred in nature, which he calls "metaphysical."

As a Kantian philosopher, he faces the difficulties entailed by any theory of metaphysical miracles, such as the phenomena of the burning bush and the crossing of the Red Sea. Breuer claims that irregularities, or so-called violations, of the laws of nature must, according to Kant's thinking, be interpreted as violations of inherently human means of cognition. Hence, despite an *a priori* readiness to accept the possible occurrence of miracles, the question arises how they can be perceived by the human mind. Breuer is therefore forced to assume that their perception by man is made possible by a divine act of grace—one might say a temporary divine award to man of additional means of cognition which make such phenomena discernible to human intelligence. Not so the metahistorical miracle manifest in the course of Jewish history; this, according to Breuer, is perceivable by the ordinary means of human cognition and as an act of divine intervention more convincing than the trite theories of scientifically oriented historians.

In view of the complexity of Breuer's distinction between metahistorical and metaphysical miracles, it may be opportune to quote his own exposition of this point.

The metaphysical miracle is not experienced by virtue of the powers of human personality, which actually has no organical means of absorbing such an experience. Newly endowed powers of perception loaned by God to man penetrate the veil of material causability and give momentary insight into the metaphysical workings of God. The experience of metaphysical miracles is essentially an act of Grace. . . .

The metahistorical miracle of the Jewish nation does not

require an act of grace in order to be experienced, nor any new
powers of cognition usually denied to mortal man. It is obvious
to the eye of reason, though it transforms the human mind into
a state of wonder.[6]

In his support of traditional Judaism, Breuer makes skillful
use of the philosophy of Kant. His gift of defense by argument,
exercised in his professional work as a lawyer, manifested itself in
language of high rhetoric spiced with undertones of irony, and
often accompanied by sudden sallies of attack and even abuse. It
was this very same gift of defense by logical argument accompanied by pathos that stood him in good stead when endeavoring to
repel the attacks upon Orthodoxy by modern trends such as
liberalism, Reform, and Zionism.

To return to Kant: the latter's distinction between phenomena
and noumena serves the purpose of demonstrating that human
knowledge is limited to the world of appearance exclusively, and is
not able to penetrate to the world of noumena—in Kant's language, the world *an sich*. The latter remains unknown to human
intelligence, constituting, in Kant's words, the eternal X, to
which human reason cannot transcend without losing the firm
basis of scientific validity.

Breuer makes use of this distinction in his attempt to defend
the traditional interpretation of the Bible against the theories of
higher criticism and a scientific approach both to such subjects
as the stories in Genesis as well as to other historical accounts in
the Scriptures whose reliability has been questioned by modern
historical and archaeological research.

Breuer's distinction between the world as creation and the
world as nature corresponds to the Kantian distinction between
noumena and phenomena. Any scientifically based contention
regarding the Scriptures has validity only in the sphere of phenomena, but not in that of noumena. However, he extends the
application of this distinction to a rather unexpected area—the
Hebrew language as such, which, he argues, is endowed with
holiness; and hence may be viewed under the aspects of both
"creation" and "nature," noumenon and phenomenon.

In other words, the contents of Scripture, rendered in Hebrew, are to human understanding mere phenomenon, which by no means exhausts its full significance. Let us hear Breuer himself on this point.

> The Holy Language belongs to God; it is both creation and nature, unlike, for instance, the German language—which originated from the German people itself. Hebrew is the repository of divine thought, and when our fathers took it over as their language they learned to think by and through it. Philologists, using their methods, view it merely as something that has evolved, and in view of existing parallels and connections (with other Semitic languages) relate it to a specific language group. Its role as the mouthpiece of God and the Word as such remains totally concealed from them.[7]

In other words, as for the noumenal content of the Bible, according to Breuer, we can never penetrate its deepest layers and be sure of gaining its ultimate meaning unless we are guided by interpretation of the Oral Law, which, being itself of divine origin, represents the surest means of unlocking its hidden implications. To be more precise on this point: Breuer admits that when the Bible narrates human situations, the principle that "The Torah speaks in human language" is perfectly valid; but whenever Scripture makes statements of a supernatural character, i.e., pertaining to acts of divine creation, revelation, or redemption, in short statements of a metaphysical nature, we can never be sure of grasping their ultimate meaning. Hence, the merely relative validity of any scientific statement about Scripture—its genesis, its content, its significance, historical accuracy, etc. Attempts to delve into the hidden core of Scripture's noumenal character, so to speak, may be found in the mystical speculations of Kabbalah, and in this context Breuer mentions the saintly author of *The Two Tablets of the Covenant*, meaning, undoubtedly, Rabbi J. H. Horowitz, who was for a time rabbi of Frankfurt at the beginning of the seventeenth century, and later moved to Safed when he joined the circle of Lurian kabbalists.

This reference to the well-known kabbalist, as well as other kabbalistic allusions in Breuer's *Der Neue Kusari*, is most significant, for it becomes clear to any perceptive reader that Breuer's latest work reveals traces of kabbalistic influence, a fact that was already diagnosed some fifty years ago by Professor Gershom Scholem in his review of *Der Neue Kusari* in the *Jüdische Rundschau*.[8]

Following Moses Mendelssohn, Breuer views Judaism mainly from the aspect of law, which to his way of thinking constitutes its essence. Hence he describes Judaism as *Gesetzesreligion*—an expression which I heard him use on more than one occasion. At other times, both in his writings and lectures, he describes the law of the Torah as *Naturrecht*,[9] meaning that it is compatible, or in harmony with, the specific nature of the Jewish people, in the sense of the biblical statement in Deuteronomy 30:14, "The word is very nigh unto thee, in thy mouth and in thy heart, that thou mayest do it."

This idea of harmony or accord between the Torah and the Jewish people (the rabbis maintain that no other nation was ever prepared to accept the Torah) finds its expression, perhaps even corroboration, in the rabbinic contention that the fathers of the Hebrew nation kept the laws of the Torah even before they were promulgated on Sinai. Of Abraham the rabbis say (*Bereshit Rabbah* 21:5) that his "kidneys exuded the Laws of Torah," which is a highly metaphorical way of saying that he "discovered," as Breuer used to say, the main body of the law of Moses by the inner light of reason and human understanding.

By describing the law of the Torah as "natural law," Breuer characterizes it as a codex that in some parts is suited to human nature in general, and *in toto* to the specific attributes of the Jewish people. In view of this idea of Breuer's, the application of the term "heteronomy" to the Judaic codex would not cover all its aspects, for this accord or harmony between the Jewish people and the Torah, on which Breuer lays such emphasis, points in the direction of autonomy rather than heteronomy.

It is surprising that this quasi-anthropological aspect of the Torah exercised so little influence on Breuer's general conception of Judaism, the more dominant feature of which, in his view, is complete heteronomy, a law commanded from above, unchangeable, and demanding total submission to it. Breuer makes this point in comparing the law of the Torah with the secular law of the gentiles. Secular law owes its existence to the State, which promulgates and enforces it. It is the sovereignty of the state which creates laws. The Jewish conception of law is entirely different, as Breuer states in the following passage:

> The Jewish nation received its law outside the country and before the foundation of the state. It achieved national unity through acceptance of the law. With this law it enters the land, with this law it founds the state: but in the midst of the state it remains the nation of the law and *it is not the state which is sovereign, but the law.* When the state broke up, the law did not crumble; and even without the state, the nation remained the nation of the law, the land remained the land of the law.[10]

This rather strange phrase of Breuer's—the sovereignty of the law—requires further elucidation. It is an expression of his vision of the Torah as, legally speaking, the supreme ruler and guide of the Jew as an individual, and in particular of the organizational set-up to which he attaches himself. In other words, the statutes of this organization have to be modeled on Halakhah in the traditional sense and solely on Halakhah, be it in the case of a Jewish community in the sense of *Kehillah*, or in the case of political party factions which nowadays play such an important role in the life of the State of Israel and which create a considerable backlash in the Diaspora.

The idea of the Torah as the sole arbiter in Jewish communal life forms the dominant feature in Breuer's conception of Judaism. He expounds on it in all his writings, in different shades, nuances, and formulations. He sometimes adds to it a dimension which might be termed philosophical, when he views the Jewish community as the materialization of the image of *Knesset Yisrael*, which arouses Platonic associations, for in Platonic thought our material world "partakes" of the qualities of ideal entities. At other times this conception seems oriented on purely Jewish ideas, when he views the organized Jewish community as a reflection of the idealized *Knesset Yisrael*, which in talmudic sources represents the Jewish people engaged in dialogue with the Almighty. The perceptive reader will even note the kabbalistic overtones with which the concept of *Knesset Yisrael* is laden in Breuer's writings. It has to be recalled that in kabbalistic thought the concept of *Knesset Yisrael* is related to the Godhead (either as an attribute or even as an integral part and almost synonymous with the Divine *Shekhina*).

A large part of Breuer's writings is taken up with the elaboration of this idea of the sovereignty of the Torah and its implications and consequences. In support of his thesis Breuer quotes relevant sources of Judaism which he interprets in a way that seem to bear out the truth of his conception. To mention just one example which I heard him cite on more than one occasion: In Deuteronomy 33:4–5 we read: "Moses commanded us a law, an inheritance of the congregation of Jacob. And there was a king in Jeshurun when the heads of the people were gathered, all the tribes of Israel together." Breuer interprets "there was a king in Jeshurun" as meaning the Torah whose sovereignty has to be acknowledged by the organized Jewish community. In other words, the Torah is its sovereign ruler.

It follows that according to Breuer any *Kehillah* or other Jewish organization which does not acknowledge the law of Torah as its constitution violates the spirit of Judaism and is therefore rejected by him. Hence, Zionism in its secular version represents, according to Breuer, a complete travesty of the essence of Judaism; but he rejects religious Zionism no less vehemently, since any cooperation with the secular majority within a political organization amounts to an acknowledgment of the latter's ideological tenets. In Breuer's words,

I recognized in Zionism the nationalism of perceptible history—the national *Yetser Hara* [evil inclination or imagination] destined to arouse the national *Yetser Hatov* [good inclination or imagination], which imbues the people of the Torah with a conscious sense of history, making them capable of action as a living nation for the first time in 2000 years and bringing them into active relation with the Land of the Torah. The *Yetser Hara* is a productive force: one cannot and one should not evade it, but one must face up to it and conquer it and force it into the service of God. It seemed to me that Orthodoxy up to that time, in its flight from the national *Yetser Hara,* had got out of line with history—denying the national element altogether and estranging itself in timid anxiety from the national home.[11]

The very term *yetser ha-ra,* as applied to Zionism, accurately reflects Breuer's attitude toward it; yet he admits that it represents a productive force by arousing the national *yetser ha-tov,* that is to say, by bringing the Jewish people back into the arena of history, from which Orthodoxy had fled because it accepted the Diaspora as its permanent destination.

It is only logical that Breuer should assume the same attitude as he does to Zionism to the Jewish community in the Diaspora (*die Grosse Gemeinde*), in which all streams of Judaism, from Reform to Orthodoxy are represented. Orthodox cooperation with such a *Kehillah* must in his view be totally rejected because, as in the case of Zionism, it entails accepting its tenets, and bestowing legitimacy upon the factions which deviate from traditional Judaism.

The controversial issue of the cooperation of Orthodoxy with modern trends of Judaism, such as liberalism and Reform, on an intracommunal basis arose in Germany a hundred years before Breuer. A highly interesting piece of evidence of this controversy is to be found in the exchange of letters on this very issue between the Rabbis Samson Raphael Hirsch, grandfather of Isaac Breuer, and Seligman Baer Bamberger, then rabbi of Würzburg. The exchange of letters was published in the fourth volume of S. R. Hirsch's selected writings.

Rabbi Hirsch decided firmly in favor of the complete autonomy of Orthodoxy, and noncooperation—at least on an intracommunal basis—with the non-Orthodox factions; whereas Rabbi Bamberger considered the separation of the Orthodox unjustified and even harmful to the Jewish community as a whole. He had, however, one reservation: that the financial contributions of the Orthodox members not be used to help support communal institutions which are contrary to Halakhah (such as organ music on Shabbat) but only those which are either shared by all trends or especially established for use of the Orthodox and in harmony with halakhic practice.

It goes without saying that the above-mentioned polemics between the two rabbis were conducted on purely halakhic grounds, both rabbis arguing their respective points in the way customary in Jewish responsa literature, basing themselves on accepted halakhic forms, i.e., relevant pronouncements or precedents in the talmudic, as well as post-talmudic, codices. Though Rabbi Bamberger suggested that the controversy be resolved by submission to a higher rabbinic authority, in the end the question remained undecided, and thus legitimacy is claimed by protagonists of both standpoints. This state of affairs need not be regretted, as it helps to create a certain amount of pluralism, which is not a disadvantage, at least if viewed in the light of modern susceptibilities.

Breuer wholeheartedly supports his grandfather's stance. However, he does not have to argue the point halakhically, as he felt this was already settled by his grandfather, but his approach might be characterized as philosophical, presenting the view of Orthodox autonomy as part of a fundamental conception of Judaism. It ought to be emphasized, however, that Breuer's writings on this point are not merely intended to present a quasi superstructure to his grandfather's halakhic stance. He was deeply convinced that his own attitude *stemmed from the essence of Judaism* as he saw it, not being able to concede legitimacy or authenticity to any other approach.

If the issue under discussion is viewed objectively, it appears that, despite Breuer's claim to merely spell out the essence of Judaism, he nevertheless creates what may be rightly termed a new ideology. This is particularly true in view of the fact that his teaching was eagerly accepted by the Agudat Israel World Organization as providing its ideological foundation. If an ideology is characterized as a rationalized defensive policy to justify and perpetuate a socioeconomic or religion-based philosophy, if this characterization is correct, it seems to suit Breuer's philosophy perfectly. To reinforce this point, it may be helpful to recall the definition of "ideology" as stated in the *International Encyclopedia of the Social Sciences*. There ideology is defined *inter alia* as

a set of ideas, relatively highly systematized or integrated around one or a few pre-eminent values. . . . It is resistant to innovations . . . and its acceptance is accompanied by highly effective overtones. Complete individual subservience to ideology is demanded of those who accept it, and it is regarded as essential and imperative that their conduct be completely permeated by it.

All these characteristics of ideology fit Breuer's stance perfectly well. We witness therefore in Breuer's work an interesting transition from Jewish philosophy to political ideology. This observation seems to me important for the following reason: in Judaism, tenets of philosophy are rarely devoid of subjective elements; being related to the realm of thought, they are not accompanied by constraints in the form of injunctions or prohibitions as to action and conduct. By their very nature they are tolerant and hospitable to divergent philosophies. Religion-based ideologies, however, may become dangerous because they are often permeated with a spirit of authoritarianism supported by the claim of divine legitimation.

There are essentially two tenets in Breuer's philosophy which form the core of his newly born ideology. Firstly, what he calls *Die Souverenität der Torah*, i.e., the claim that the Torah, not the Jewish people, is sovereign. Secondly, that only a community which accepts the law of the Torah as its constitution is endowed with historical legitimacy and worthy of representing and reflecting *Knesset Yisrael*, whatever the latter's interpretation. According to Breuer, those who reject these two principles place themselves outside the pale of the Holy Congregation of Israel, and they are the ones to be regarded as separatists, and not the adherents of autonomous Orthodoxy.

Neither of the two claims created a significant stir in the Jewish world. The first, possibly, because its meaning is rather obscure, and its implications not sufficiently manifest; the second, because it was identified with the well-known separatist views held at the time by Orthodox rabbis in various European countries and therefore did not constitute an innovation in Jewish religious life. However, when the first tenet, claiming that the Torah and not the Jewish people was sovereign, was adopted at the first Knessiah Gedolah of Agudat Israel, which took place in Vienna in

1923, it was strongly criticized by Dr. H. P. Chajes, then Chief Rabbi of Vienna. In a sermon which he delivered on September 11, 1923, he referred to this resolution in the following words:

> My friends, it is my duty to warn you of an imminent serious danger, whose equal has not been experienced by our people for a long time. I am referring to two resolutions of the Knessiah Gedolah, which constitute a menace to the spirit of our Judaism. First, that not the people, but only the Torah is sovereign. Second, that the community does not elect a lay leadership, but is represented by a Council of Rabbis who are guided by the will of the Torah.[12]

As to the first point, relating to the sovereignty of the Torah, Rabbi Chajes maintains that if translated into actual fact it would mean spiritual enslavement. Moreover, he claims, the relationship between God and the people of Israel is symbolized by the Covenant, which presupposes the sovereignty of the Jewish people. "This Covenant is so deeply rooted in the people's consciousness that God is even admonished to adhere to its terms." As for the second resolution criticized by Rabbi Chajes, it would appear to me that this simply indicates neotheocratic rule of the organization of Agudat Israel. It should be noted that both resolutions are the spiritual offspring of Isaac Breuer's ideology.[13]

Notwithstanding Rabbi Chajes's criticism, I do not wish to contend in principle that the foundation of autonomous Orthodox communities is always to be deplored. Separate establishments of this kind may be justified on purely pragmatic grounds if they eliminate, or at least mitigate, intracommunal strife and help to create a strong Jewish milieu which is culturally and educationally productive. Such "separation" may be particularly justified if it does not preclude close cooperation on an extracommunal basis with other trends in Judaism. What seems to me open to criticism is the attempt to support such separation by an ideology which by its very nature is impervious to change and burdened with nuances of an overbearing authoritarianism.

With the decline of ideologies of any kind in our time, the Jewish philosophy of Isaac Breuer has lost much of the appeal which it had in the past for some sections of the Jewish communities. Moreover, the type of Judaism mirrored in his writings cannot be regarded as attractive if judged by any standard valid in our time. The great importance that Breuer attaches to organizational allegiance is no longer shared by contemporary Jews. We tend to judge loyalty to Judaism by different criteria; authenticity and sincerity of faith, moral conduct as well as religious observance. "Tell me to what Jewish organization you belong, and I shall tell you what kind of Jew you are" is a maxim of very narrow validity.

In some ways Breuer's philosophy is remindful of the religious conceptions adopted by the sect of Neturei Karta, a fossilized relic of medieval times. It cannot be denied that the extremism of Breuer's ideology—as reflected in his writings more than in his political activities—goes beyond the policy generally adopted by Agudat Israel in its relation to the State of Israel. The Agudah's attitude to the crucial problem of cooperation with *Medinat Yisrael* is guided by halakhic considerations as promulgated by its Council of Sages. It has already been pointed out that Halakhah tends to be less rigid than ideological tenets and more adaptable to the exigencies of changing times. It must be noted, however, in fairness to Breuer, that unlike Neturei Karta, he was a man of the world imbued with European culture. Yet the pervasive vein of theocracy, albeit in westernized form, which characterizes his philosophy, aligns it with the ideology of that group. The tenets drawn from Jewish sources are garnished by Breuer with a varied assortment of influences, ranging from Samson Raphael Hirsch to Kabbalah, from Plato to Kant, Stammler, and Schopenhauer. In his review article of *Der Neue Kuzari*, mentioned above, Gershom Scholem already drew attention to the diverse character of Breuer's spiritual and intellectual mentors.

A further factor which has contributed to the obsolescence of Breuer's views is his unbounding faith in the truth of Kant's philosophy. It is amazing that a man with such an acute mind was capable of accepting Kant's philosophical position as final truth. This he did despite the fact that already in his time and within Germany there was extant a body of literature critical of

Kant, not to mention the criticisms launched against Kant out-side Germany, emanating *inter alia* from the lectures and writings of Franz Brentano, as well as the so-called Vienna circle of philosophy. The following quotation from Breuer shows the extent of his admiration of Kant:

> God caused to rise among the nations the exceptional man Kant, who, on the basis of the Socratic and Cartesian skepticism, brought about that "Copernican turn," whereby the whole of man's reasonings was set in steel limits within which alone perception is legitimized. Blessed be God who, in His wisdom, created Kant! Every real Jew who seriously and honestly studies the "Critique of Pure Reason," is bound to pronounce his "Amen" on it.[14]

That a man so highly gifted and endowed with such a rich mind should—metaphorically speaking—have landed himself in an intellectual cul-de-sac, calls for some explanation. Three factors may have brought about this rather sad state of affairs. First, Isaac Breuer was born in Hungary. The tradition of uncompromising Hungarian-Jewish Orthodoxy—the *ecclesia militans* of world Jewry during the first decades of this century—was transmitted to him by his father, Rabbi Solomon Breuer. Secondly, this tradition was reinforced by the spiritual legacy of Breuer's maternal grandfather, Rabbi Samson Raphael Hirsch. The personality of the latter exercised a particular fascination for his grandson, and became the basis of what might be characterized as a grandfather fixation. Finally, we notice in Breuer's writings signs of a Germanic infatuation with ideology. His writings disclose a mentality close to that state of mind so aptly expressed by the Latin saying *fiat iustitia, pereat mundus.* A confluence of these three factors may, at least to some extent, explain the contrast between the elaborate construction and sophistication of Breuer's philosophical system and its disappointing outcome in practical terms.

In fairness to Breuer it has to be admitted that his writings also contain a number of progressive elements which should not be ignored. We have noted that his mind was always open to consider, assess, and if possible absorb ideas emanating from non-Jewish philosophies. On the whole, and notwithstanding the ideological implications of his writings, his conception of Judaism was marked by the motto *Torah im derekh erez* in its widest possible sense. The inherently agonistic tendency of his thought also deserves to be singled out for praise. In subsequent chapters of this book more will be said about his attitude to higher criticism of the Bible, to the problem of faith and doubt, and his important role in shaping a modernized Orthodox Jewish outlook in general. Finally, since I have characterized his anti-Zionist ideology as unattractive, I wish to add that this epithet by no means applies to Breuer's personality. He was outgoing and generous, particularly in relation to young people, a brilliant conversationalist, a lavish entertainer, and the most impressive orator I have ever heard.

I should like to support this last point by the following observation of a very outspoken adversary of Isaac Breuer on ideological grounds, the German Zionist leader Kurt Blumenfeld, who, nevertheless, was deeply impressed by Breuer when attending his lectures in Frankfurt-am-Main.

In Frankfurt, a rain of arrows was shot at us from every corner, and the accusation was voiced that Zionism blunts the Messianic doctrine of Judaism. However, I found there among the Orthodox opponents of Zionism one important voice, that of Isaac Breuer. He defended his views with such adroitness and subtlety that I had to listen to his lectures with both interest and appreciation. After one such lecture of his, I approached him in order to thank him. "Why are you of all people thanking me?" he asked. I replied, "Amongst those whom you did not convince, there is not one on whom you have made a deeper impression."[15]

4

Traditional Judaism in Modern Garb: The Jewish Philosophy of Yeshayahu Leibowitz

Yeshayahu Leibowitz, professor of organic chemistry, medical doctor, and possessor of a host of other academic qualifications, is a well-known, though controversial, figure on the Israeli scene and a favorite of the Israeli media. He has gained this popularity because of his intellectual stature, his colorful personality, and his fierce nonconformism in matters of politics and religion. Young people in particular are fascinated by his extreme outspokenness and candor, his sardonic temper, and his iconoclasmic outbursts. Apart from his purely scientific record, he has not published extensively except in the years since his retirement from official academic duties. Most of his work is embodied in the *Hebrew Encyclopedia*, of which he was chief editor for many years. His essays on matters of Judaism, Jewish philosophy, and the Jewish state are published in three volumes, the first of which is called *Torah u-Mitzvot Basman ha-Zeh* ("Torah and Commandments in Our Time"), published by Massada, Tel-Aviv, in 1954; the second *Yahadut, Am Yehudi u-Medinat Yisrael* ("Judaism, the Jewish People, and the State of Israel"), published by Schocken, Tel-Aviv, in 1976; and the last *Emunah, Historiah ve-Arakhim* ("Faith, History, and Values"), published by Akademon,

Jerusalem, in 1982. All his books are collections of essays, articles, and short pieces published previously in Hebrew dailies or periodicals. His philosophical writing is extremely lucid, free from the pedantries and obfuscations of professional philosophers. His ideas, few in number, are simple, coherent, and mostly of a fundamental character. The relative paucity of ideas and the frequent recapitulation of them by the author, both orally and in writing, make it possible to sum them up and discuss them under a number of headings, which I shall explicate one by one. These are: privatization, demystification, desacralization, theocentricism, disengagement or separation of religion and science, of religion and history, of religion and ethics, and of state and synagogue.

"Privatized" Judaism, is, according to Leibowitz, by no means an ideal, but rather the outcome of the fact that its most essential feature—Halakhah—is on the whole of an exilic character, presupposing, as it does, the existence of Jewish communities dispersed in gentile environments. In other words, most of the Halakhah was compiled and adopted long before the establishment of an independent Jewish state was envisioned, and hence the possibility that it would one day be called upon to become the law of a state was never considered. Leibowitz maintains that Halakhah is at present in a frozen state, which may be an exaggeration, but there is obviously more than a grain of truth in his contention, since the "thawing" of Halakhah has proceeded very slowly indeed, and has not kept pace with the requirements of a modern state.

In view of the fact that Halakhah is not sufficiently developed to cope with the problems of a Jewish state, Leibowitz has ceased, in his later writings, to advocate its incorporation into the law of the state by way of parliamentary legislation. Thus, his conception of Judaism has undergone a change, moving, as it does, in the direction of what may be called "privatization." At present it appeals exclusively to individual choice and conviction, carefully avoiding anything that might be termed religious coercion. On this point Leibowitz is in line with modern tendencies in the religious life of other denominations.

There are many Israelis who are to some extent and in one way

or another influenced by Leibowitz; his more faithful followers are
members of the Israeli academic community, to whom his selec-
tion of a number of religious themes and the molding of them into
a coherent system of ultimate significance exercises a strong
appeal.

Demystification

Leibowitz's Jewish philosophy has a pronounced rational tinge.
In a certain sense his philosophic ancestors are Maimonides, and
of more recent vintage, Moses Mendelssohn and Isaac Breuer. It
will be recalled that the last two viewed Judaism as *Gesetzes-
Religion*—a religion established and mainly characterized by religious law. Leibowitz's philosophy is miles removed from any
school of thought which views Judaism as based on mystical
experience or mere religious feelings of any kind. His views and
those of Buber, for instance, for whom Judaism is mainly religious faith of a particular character, are completely antithetical.
Nor has he much use for the historical phenomenon of Hassid-
ism, neither in its original nor its modernized fashion. He reveals
no liking for the various streams of Jewish mysticism and the
Jewish messianic or quasi-messianic movements, to the explora-
tion of which the late Gershom Scholem devoted a lifetime of
study and research. Needless to say, he does not in any way
denigrate faith, which in the view of many philosophers of Judaism forms the basis of Jewish religious life. But it is by no means
in the foreground of his religious conception, which is dominated
by what might be termed commitment, *avodat Hashem* expressed in the fulfillment of mitzvot. Not without reason has this
type of Judaism been characterized as "behavioristic."

Desacralization

Avodah zarah—idolatry—is Leibowitz's main bugbear. He shows
no reverence toward holy places, not even the Wailing Wall,
deemed sacred by so many Jews, religious and secular. He calls it
"a pile of stones constructed by the wicked King Herod." Indeed,
he denies religious or any other significance to the alleged holy

character of the land of Israel, declaring emphatically and on countless occasions that the epithet "holy" may only be applied to the disciplined and saintly conduct of human beings who master their desires and inclinations and serve the Lord by leading a life of Torah and mitzvot. This desacralization of Judaism runs parallel to similar trends in Christian religious thought. The Yale professor of philosophy of religion, Louis Dupré, writes in a Leibowitzian vein when, in an essay entitled "Spiritual Life in a Secular Age," he says: "Today, the 'sacred' wherever it is still experienced, has lost the power to integrate directly the rest of life. We are now witnessing the unprecedented phenomenon of a religion that is rapidly becoming desacralized. The experience of the sacred with which phenomenologists since Rudolph Otto have readily identified religion can no longer be considered normative of the religion of our time."[1] It is mainly on account of these two trends—demystification and desacralization—that Leibowitz is regarded as a religious iconoclast, a demolisher of common religious conventions and prejudices in the name of what he considers to be a Judaism of strict observance of Torah and mitzvot.

Theocentricity

Leibowitz defines theocentricity as a conception which regards the observance of the Torah commandments as the most fundamental tenet of Judaism—and so much so that he practically equalizes Judaism with a set of mitzvot observed by Jews throughout the ages on which certain religious tenets of faith are superimposed. It is the observance of mitzvot that creates faith rather than the other way around. Moreover, the concept of theocentricity incorporates the idea that service to the Lord has to be rendered neither out of fear of divine retribution nor in the expectation of reward in this world or the world-to-come. Leibowitz rejects a philosophy of Judaism modeled on the theories of the many theologians and sociologists who justify religion as good for man, helping him to attain individual happiness, self-fulfillment, spiritual elevation, psychological support, or to fulfill any overt or covert need or desire. Anyone who serves the Lord because he believes that religion bestows upon him such benefits does not serve God but is actually serving himself. Religion in the service of man is anthropocentric, just as service to the Lord is theocentric. "What can I get out of Judaism?" is an irrelevant question which should not be asked by a true believer. A truly religious Jew would ask himself, "What am I duty bound to do in order to serve my Lord?" The following passage—one of many— from Leibowitz's book amply substantiates this point.

> Any justification of the commandments by the human needs they are to fulfill, or any attempt to base them on human desires or strivings, intellectual, moral, social, or national, empties them of religious meaning, for if the commandments are an expression of some philosophic thought, or if they are meant to improve society or help to preserve the Jewish people, then he who upholds them does not serve the Lord but himself, society, or his people. . . . he uses the divine Torah for his own benefit and as a means to satisfy his own needs.[2]

As will be seen, this theocentric conception of religion has its antecedents in Jewish as well as Christian thought. It must be stated, however, that complete rejection of humanistic elements in Judaism is rare in the history of Jewish philosophy, yet it is characteristic of Leibowitz's thought, constituting one of the outstanding principles of his sharply defined ideas.

It is quite possible that Leibowitz's strong emphasis on service to the Lord as the very heart of Judaism, and his somewhat contemptuous attitude to the widespread feeling—particularly among sociologists—that "religion is good for you," hence "Judaism is good for the Jew," springs from his love of sharp antithetical juxtaposition of ideas: in the case under discussion, theocentricity versus anthropocentricity. As a matter of fact, he does not, and actually cannot, reject sincere religious conduct, no matter what its motivation may be. He is, after all, fully aware of the many scriptural passages and rabbinical sayings which may be characterized as "anthropocentric." They are legion, and there is no need to quote them here. Suffice it to mention one of the most illuminating talmudic sayings apparently contradicting Leibowitz's thesis: "Let a man occupy himself with study of the Torah and fulfillment of commandments, although he do so not out of love of the Lord; for the consequence may be that he will do so with true sincerity and faith" (*Pesachim* 50b).

Professor Leibowitz, of course, knows all the sources which apparently contradict his thesis; yet he firmly upholds it, emphasizing, as he does, the enormous superiority of religious conduct *lishmo*—out of love of the Lord—over such conduct *shelo lishmo.* By doing so he follows his admired mentor Maimonides, whose views he presents in a somewhat Leibowitzian interpretation. It cannot be denied that there is genuine religious feeling in this extreme demand for complete subservience to God out of pure love, in the sense of "Thou shalt love the Lord thy God with all thine heart, with all thy soul, and with all thy might."

Disengagement or Separation

According to Leibowitz, the essence of Judaism is incorporated in its halakhic content. It follows that the narrative of the Bible, the historical background depicted therein, the whole framework of facts, occurrences, and their chronological sequence are, in the view of Leibowitz, elements of minor significance, and their accuracy or inaccuracy in the light of modern research of extrabiblical sources is irrelevant. The Torah's purpose is not to teach history to mankind. Moreover, argues Leibowitz somewhat surprisingly, history, including that of the Jewish people, is of no religious significance. He goes so far as to claim that historical events have little lasting impact on the religious consciousness of man. He says: "We learn from the Torah and the prophets that what is presented in these sources as the revelation of God to man did not firmly implant religious faith in the children of Israel."[3] To corroborate this, Leibowitz draws attention to the fact that the incident of the golden calf followed shortly after the divine revelation on Mount Sinai. He also regards as a witness Moses, who said shortly before his death: "For I know thy rebellion and thy stiff neck: behold, while I am yet alive with you this day ye have been rebellious against the Lord, and how much more after my death."

The miraculous events that, according to the biblical account, occurred to the Jewish people could not prevent the frequent relapses of the Jews into crude customs of idolatry, with all their immoral manifestations. The conclusion drawn by Leibowitz from these events is that there is no direct connection between what happens in history and the religious consciousness of man. In other words, the impact of certain occurrences upon the life of a people does not necessarily influence the course of their lives, nor does this impact affect the deepest levels of consciousness. According to Leibowitz, the acceptance of Judaism is the individual act of a person who makes a decision in favor of allegiance to Torah, and it is rarely affected by events in the external world. But this, I think, is an overstatement, for in actual fact we cannot help being influenced by so-called external events. Leibowitz is probably right, however, in asserting that external events rarely affect us in only one direction, and that much depends upon the psychic make-up of the individual.

According to Leibowitz, faith and religious commitment are, as a rule, the outcome of processes within the soul, and more often than not uninfluenced by historical events. This idea forms the gist of Leibowitz's attempt to deprive history of its function as religious catalyst, and, indeed, he goes so far as to claim that, religiously speaking, history is of no significance whatsoever. This disengagement of history and religion may very well serve the purpose of releasing the tensions and solving the conflicts that result from viewing the biblical narrative in the light of modern historical research. In other words, having "debunked" attachment to the religious significance of history in general, including the biblical narrative, Leibowitz feels no need to argue with or inveigh against modern historical research or consider its bearing on the genesis of the Jewish religion.

In a similar vein Leibowitz approaches the important confrontation between religion and science. It has to be recalled that he believes that it is the halakhic content of the Bible that forms the heart of Judaism and that the Bible has to be viewed in the light of its oral interpretation (*Torah she-be-al-peh*). It is on the basis of this that the twenty-four books were included in the Holy Canon, which demonstrates the dominance of oral tradition over the written text. Moreover, if the divine commandments are explicated by their oral interpretation, the written version alone may not convey their ultimate meaning. It follows that the surface wording of the Bible is of minor significance and should not be accepted literally. Hence, a confrontation between, say, the Genesis story about the creation of the world and that of creative evolution or any other modern scientific theory makes no sense, since the biblical account and scientific method fall into different categories. If I may quote a Czech proverb, I might say, in the spirit of Leibowitz, that comparing the Bible with scientific theory is like comparing the sky to bagpipes. To quote Leibowitz, "It is the aim of Torah and Holy Writ to determine man's place before God and the obedience due to Him, not to impart knowledge about the world, nature, history, not even about man himself."[4] Such statements are, of course, legion in Leibowitz's writings: "The Bible is a holy book belonging to a category fundamentally different from any textbook on biology, geology, or any of the sciences." Hence we are thoroughly mistaken if we relate to it as if it were a scientific textbook; and a further quotation from the same essay: "The Torah is no source of scientific information, but aims to instill in us fear of the Lord, love of the Lord, and service to the Lord."[5]

As in the case of history versus Torah, so in the case of science versus Torah: the attempt at disengagement, whether successful or not, is, I conjecture, a means of preventing or repelling possible attacks upon religion by science. In other words, Leibowitz claims that there need be no confrontation between them because of the fundamental differences between the conceptual systems, methodologies, and aims of the two spheres. Therefore we may concede to science the truth of its findings without calling into question the truth of religion. We may perhaps describe this tendency of Leibowitz as one highly characteristic of his thought, namely, his desire to resolve contradictions by logical distinction. This tendency becomes manifest in his propensity to draw a clear line of separation between religion and its potential or real adversaries, claiming that they lack the *tertium comparationis.* In Leibowitz's somewhat metaphoric expression, the divine *Shekhinah* did not descend on Mount Sinai in order to teach us history and science, but to teach us how to serve the Lord. In Leibowitz's opinion, a

masterly summary of the ultimate intent of Torah is contained in
the following two verses of Deuteronomy:

> And now, Israel, what does the Lord thy God require of thee, but
> to fear the Lord thy God, to walk in all His ways and to love Him,
> and to serve the Lord thy God with all thy heart, with all thy
> soul. To keep the commandments of the Lord and His statutes
> which I command thee this day for thy good?

Ethics and Religion

As with science and religion and with history and religion,
ethics, too, is disengaged from religion in Leibowitz's philosophy.
According to Leibowitz, these two are often contradictory. Philosophic ethics is anthropocentric, humanistic; religion—to give
precision to Leibowitz's exposition of it—is theocentric. Ethics is
autonomous; religion is heteronomous, or, better still, theono-
mous. There are certain divine commands in the Bible that run
counter to our ethical consciousness, such as Samuel's killing of
Agag, king of Amalek, when the latter was already a defenseless
prisoner, the binding of Isaac, or the story of Job, which also raise
questions of an ethical nature. It is possible that Leibowitz's
conception of the relationship or nonrelationship between ethics
and religion is in accordance with, or, perhaps, is even an echo of,
the philosophy of Soren Kierkegaard, who viewed religion and
ethics as antinomian and therefore placed the religious stage in
the life of man above the ethical.

If one accepts Leibowitz's suppositions, then humanism, viewing man per se as of ultimate value and the service of man as an
"ought"—a moral obligation—and religion, viewing man exclusively as a servant of the Lord, and such service as a "must," are
antithetical, and irreconcilable. It is hardly surprising, therefore,
that the very concept of religious humanism is highly questionable in Leibowitz's view, and he does not mention it, not even as a
possible alternative to his viewpoint. Thus, he parts company,
though rather circumspectly, with his former colleagues at the
Hebrew University, namely, the late Martin Buber and Hugo
Bergman as well as Ernst Simon, all of whom are adherents of a

Jewish philosophy the common denominator of which may, in broad terms, be described as a certain kind of religious humanism.

State and Religion

It has already been stated that Leibowitz's demand for separation between the state and religion stems from the rigidity and inviolateness of Halakhah, the compilers of which never envisaged its relevance to a sovereign Jewish state. This being so, there is no possibility of establishing a *Medinat haTorah*, with Halakhah as its legal foundation. In countless pronouncements, both written and oral, Leibowitz gives vent to his dislike of what appears in everyday life in modern Israel. The government's patronage of certain religious rites and customs which have been adopted as state laws, whether out of the need for pleasing, placating, or satisfying the Orthodox minority in order to secure its support of the perennial coalition, or out of a desire to give the secular state a few of the trappings of Jewish lore to underpin the claim of historical continuity and authenticity—all this is, in Leibowitz's view, humiliating to both Judaism and the religious community. On this issue, he agrees with the protagonists of extreme secularism, advocating the disestablishment of traditional Judaism in the State of Israel, and demanding that religious Jewry organize itself in independent congregations under their own leadership, preferably unsupported by the state. He believes that only a proud and independent religious Jewry will command the respect of the whole nation, and will acquire the moral stature to be an effective critic and even an antagonist of the secular state. The main goal of religious Jewry will then be to fight for the transformation of the secular state into a *Medinat ha-Torah*, which is Leibowitz's ultimate ideal, assuming hopefully that in the course of time Halakhah will become flexible enough to be suitable for adoption as state law. It does not matter to him how long it takes to achieve this goal, nor is he sure that it will ever be achieved, but the very process of striving toward it appears to him both necessary and valuable.

We may put aside the question of whether a separation so

radical and clear-cut is feasible from a practical point of view. Even if one supposes that the Orthodox community of Israel would be prepared to accept Leibowitz's extreme viewpoint, would it be economically strong enough to maintain its own religious institutions, including a complete and variegated school system, catering for roughly one-third of Israeli youth, from kindergarten to yeshiva, kollel, and university? One point is certain surely: Leibowitz does not object to the complete polarization of the population of Israel and its division into two communities, secular and religious. He has no compunction about such a dichotomy; on the contrary, he views it as desirable; he does not shrink from its possible consequences: confrontation leading to conflict and not necessarily exclusively in the intellectual sphere.[6]

It must be mentioned that Leibowitz welcomes conflict as such, claiming that it acts as a powerful stimulus to progress, and will help to bring about a true renaissance of Jewish religious life. In his own words:

> The separation of religion and state, i.e., the withdrawal of religion from the administrative framework of a secular regime, is tantamount to the demolishing of the religious ghetto walls that were erected in the state of Israel; it is a breach in the sphere that was allotted to the Jewish religion by the secular state, and which official religious Jewry is reluctant to leave. After the separation, the independent religious communities and their institutions will stand vis-à-vis the secular reality with dignity, being no longer a tolerated part of it. Then there will follow an intellectual, educational, social, and political struggle—an open struggle—for Torah in all the spheres of life within the nation and the state.[7]

Antecedents

The theocentrism which Leibowitz advocates so vociferously was not his invention, nor is this term his exclusive coinage. As a matter of fact, theocentrism is one of the characteristics of the theology of Luther. According to the German theologian Erich Schaeder, who published a book called *Theocentric Theology* (vol.

I in 1909, vol. II in 1914),[8] religion originates in the concept of God rather than in man. The concept of the Godhead emphasizes His might and sovereign rights and ordinances rather than His love. In a similar spirit, the German Evangelical theologian Karl Holl (1866–1926), who taught at the University of Tübingen, became the spokesman of a theology whose characteristic theme was theocentric thought, based on two central assumptions: (1) that the concept of God is not to be understood as issuing from man, but rather the opposite, that man is to be judged and measured by the concept of God, and (2) that the motivation toward religion is not to be sought in the needs and desires of man, but in the duties imposed upon him by God.

Needless to say, we cannot be sure that Leibowitz knew one or both of these theologians, despite the fact that his views are congruent with theirs. Being a scholar of encyclopedic knowledge and, in a way, an encyclopedist himself, Leibowitz might have been acquainted with their writings, particularly in view of the fact that both Schaeder and Holl taught at German universities in the days when Leibowitz was a student.

Among the other non-Jewish influences on Leibowitz one might mention, first and foremost, Immanuel Kant, whose philosophy dominated the intellectual life of Germany in Leibowitz's formative years. Kant's ethical rigor, his insistence on complete disinterestedness in human conduct, his refusal to regard man's actions as moral in the fullest sense unless motivated by a sense of duty (*aus Pflicht*), not from personal inclination or self-interest—all this may have influenced Leibowitz in his emphatic insistence on disinterested service to the Lord. If the German philosopher Arthur Schopenhauer is right in claiming that Kant's ethics represents a transformation or, rather, transposition of the rigorous religious demands of the Old Testament (Kant's father was a Protestant clergyman) into a quasi-secular, humanistic, and autonomous system of ethics—if this assumption is correct—we might say that Leibowitz, by a reversal of Kant's thinking process, returned the rigor to its original source, namely, religion.

Kierkegaard's possible influence on Leibowitz has already been mentioned and was suggested by some of Leibowitz's disciples. The idea of the complete separation of ethics from religion was

prominently advocated by Leibowitz, but it was a suggestion so
audacious that had he not been fortified by antecedents such as
Kierkegaard, there is some doubt that he would have proposed
such a separation.

As might be expected, the influence of Jewish philosophers on
Leibowitz is even more marked than that of non-Jewish ones. I
have already stated that in more than one respect Maimonides
was his guiding light. I find, however, that of all the Jewish
philosophers, his strongest affinity—conscious or no—is with
Moses Mendelssohn. Both view Halakhah, historically speaking,
as the most pervasive and dominant feature of Judaism; both aim
at making accommodations with modern intellectual develop-
ments outside the world of Judaism; both view Judaism not as an
isolated historical spiritual phenomenon but as related to and,
indeed, embedded in the wider context of human civilization;
both strongly advocate the separation of state and religion. Both,
in a definite sense, are religious reductionists operating within
the realm of traditional Judaism. Mendelssohn sacrificed the
specific character of Jewish religious faith to the outdated belief
that faith is related to reason, which is of a universal character
and not specifically Jewish. And Leibowitz sacrificed his belief in
the historical and scientific accuracy of Holy Writ to, it may be
assumed, the accommodation of Judaism to the twentieth-cen-
tury outlook and, from a practical point of view, to make it
possible for an observant Jew to pursue any scientific activity
without getting involved in insoluble contradictions and conflicts.

Since the phenomena of faith and religious experience do not
play an important role in the thought of Leibowitz, it may be
argued that his philosophy of Judaism is unattractive and unlikely to draw the Jewish skeptic and unbeliever into the orbit of
traditional Judaism. I recall that, according to Leibowitz, serving
the Lord in the way required by traditional Judaism is a matter of
individual decision, and here the question arises why a Jewish
person should decide to take upon himself the task of serving the
Lord by keeping the commandments of Torah. Leibowitz might
possibly answer that in any case a choice has to be made between
serving the Lord and serving some manner of secular cult not far

removed from idolatry, with all the questionable morality which is bound up with the latter choice. Leibowitz is an inveterate pessimist as far as the good in human nature is concerned. His favorite motto concerning human nature is from chapter 6 of Genesis, "And the Lord saw that the wickedness of man was great on the earth and that every imagination of the thoughts of his heart was only evil continually."

By committing himself to service to the Lord, the Jew may learn how to redeem himself from this continual flow of evil thoughts and inclinations. Leibowitz, however, because he denigrates any kind of religious utilitarianism, cannot argue in this way, because such motivation has a utilitarian ring. If neither faith nor religious experience nor lessons drawn from Jewish history constitute paths leading to Judaism, then why can service to the Lord be done only and exclusively through Torah and mitzvot?

And so it may be argued that Leibowitz's philosophy is more likely to offer psychological support and intellectual succor to a Jew who by birth or nurture, or both, is already within the purview of traditional Judaism. The strongest and most refreshing point of Leibowitz's philosophy, however, is his attempt to come to terms with the modern scientific ideas which are so pervasive in our present-day life. He does so by conceding to them their relative truth, and, thus, keeping traditional Jewish life free of conflict.

Viewing his work in a wider perspective, one must admit that his interpretation of traditional Judaism—in spite of the many objections that could be raised to it, some of which have not been dealt with in this chapter—represents a novel and audacious attempt to come to terms with the problems and perplexities of the modern Jew, made from inside Orthodoxy.

Facets of Modernity

5

Faith and Doubt

No discourse on doubt as a religious problem is to be found in rabbinic literature. The Hebrew word *safek* ("doubt") is generally used in a halakhic context: there may, for instance, be doubt concerning the marital status of a person. If a man disappears in the course of war, doubt will arise as to whether he is alive or dead; similarly *safek* may arise about the use of foodstuffs in the kitchen. Needless to say, halakhic doubts coming into notice in the course of Jewish life are legion and are amply dealt with in Talmud and codes. Naturally, there is also ample evidence of the rabbis' dealing with matters of actual sin in the sense of transgression of law, whether individual or social, including serious issues such as sectarianism, subversive treason, and apostasy, but doubt in matters of religious doctrine, in contradistinction to actual rejection of fundamental tenets of Judaism, does not per se rank as a problem in the view of the rabbis.

Let us consider the well-known case of Elisha ben Abuya, a great rabbinic scholar and teacher of Rabbi Meir (third generation of tannaim), who became an apostate and was hence dubbed Aḥer ("another," "a stranger"). The Talmud shows great interest in elucidating this defection. According to one account, a profound mystical or theosophic experience might have led Elisha ben Abuya to believe in two divinities, and he may thus possibly be guilty of the heresy of dualism (*Ḥagigah* 15a). Another account has it that he saw a youngster climbing a tree with the intention of chasing the mother -bird away before taking her young, as the Torah commands, promising "that it may be well with thee, that thou mayest prolong thy days." (Deuteronomy 22:6). And yet as he watched, the youngster fell and was killed. And yet another explanation is that during the time of the Hadrianic persecution Elisha ben Abuya saw the tongue of Ḥuẓpit the Interpreter—a saintly scholar who had been martyred—dragged along by a pig. Exclaiming, "The mouth that uttered pearls licks the dust," he went forth and sinned (*Kiddushin* 19b).

The variety of explanations advanced for the apostasy of Elisha ben Abuya seems to indicate that the rabbis were deeply perturbed by this manifestation and anxious to understand its underlying psychological motives. However, they did not view his apostasy as the culmination of an intermediate state of doubt (although this probably was the case), but explained it as a sudden reversal of previous faith brought about by the pressure of unusual and shattering experiences.

The nonoccurrence of doubt in rabbinic literature does not point to the absence of psychological understanding. Many of the rabbis' deliberations on the lives of men, the motives for their conduct, their strivings and reactions to various human situations, even their legal ordinances and rules show intuitive psychological insight of a high degree. However, in times of faith, a belief in God and other such metaphysical contentions were regarded as natural facts, much as we regard factual knowledge in modern times. Regarding Jewish doctrine, belief in God is emphasized in the first of the Ten Commandments, interpreted by Nachmanides and other commentators as having positive import, enjoining us to believe in God "who brought thee out of the land of Egypt, out of the house of bondage." Finally, even if we assume that the problem of religious doubt did occur, the rabbis did not regard it as worth expressing, particularly since, as men of profound religious conviction, they were reluctant to draw attention to it.

According to Rabbi Norman Lamm, the very first and perhaps only Jewish thinker who discussed doubt as such was Rabbi Sa'adia Gaon in the introduction to his *Book of Doctrines and Beliefs*.[1] This is consistent with the rational nature of Sa'adia's philosophical approach, in particular his belief that the doctrinal principles of Judaism—unity of God, revelation, creation, future life—can be demonstrated by reason. Hence there is no fundamental difference between metaphysical propositions and normal, matter-of-fact knowledge. If a man harbors doubts about a doctrinal tenet of Judaism, it is merely an indication that he has not sufficiently clarified his ideas and eliminated errors from his thinking. In other words, doubt is a symptom of faulty or imperfect reasoning. To quote Sa'adia himself: "Let not therefore the fool in his impatience lay the blame for his own faults on the Creator by saying that He implanted these doubts in him, whereas it is his own ignorance or impatience which threw him into confusion."[2] Sa'adia, then, sees religious doubt as a natural concomitant of any learning process, and capable of being removed by sound instruction and diligent application.

Jewish religious philosophy in modern times has more to say about religious doubt, though the references are still infrequent, particularly among Orthodox thinkers. Doubt as such did not loom large in the religious writings of Moses Mendelssohn, because he, like Sa'adia, regarded metaphysical verities as grounded in reason, and therefore religious doubt, in his view, is no different from doubt of a cognitive nature. However only a few generations later, Isaac Breuer seems to have been personally involved in the phenomenon of doubt and deals with it in depth in some of his writings.[3]

Breuer distinguishes between Judaism as law and Judaism as doctrine (*Lehre*), by which he means the principles of faith underlying the law. On doctrine he has *inter alia* the following to say:

> The Jew approaches the doctrine of Judaism—as of course any doctrine—as an examiner, but the law ensures that he does not pass judgment on the doctrine, but on himself. The law constraints the Jew to interpret every incongruity between a person and doctrine as a failing in the person and therefore not to reject the doctrine but to educate himself.[4]

In essence, Breuer claims that obedience to law should not be dependent upon doctrine—that is to say, religious faith—and he views coexistence of both faith and practice of law as the final goal. It follows that religious doubt per se is not an evil, for the very reason that it need not endanger the doubter's allegiance to Judaism. As Breuer puts it, "the more absolute the obedience which the law demands, the more room there is in Judaism for the soul that is wrestling for knowledge and truth."[5]

An even more positive function of religious doubt emerges in the concluding paragraph of Breuer's essay "Law and the Individual," summed up in this strikingly picturesque passage: "The storm waves of doubt must dash themselves against the immovable dam of the law in order to fertilize in well-defined boundaries the soil from which the miraculous flower of free conviction is to spring forth."[6]

Two points require comment: First, by referring to free religious conviction as a "miraculous" manifestation, Breuer reveals the uphill path he himself had to climb before reaching the pinnacle of firm religious belief. Second, Breuer, like other modern Orthodox thinkers, such as Isaiah Leibowitz, demands unquestioning obedience to Halakhah, even in the face of doubt. It is this fact that protects the doubter from defection from Judaism until such time as the "miraculous flower of free conviction" takes root. To encourage the emergence of religious conviction is, according to Breuer, one of the main tasks of religious education or self-education.

The problem of religious doubt emerges again in a later work by Breuer—a philosophical novel portraying the life of German-Jewish academic youth in the first decades of this century. In the course of a night scene in which two German-Jewish youths engage in a tense and emotionally charged discussion on religious topics, the Orthodox Berthold—one of the main figures in the novel—admits to being tormented by religious doubts concerning the Jewish faith. When asked by his friend why he nevertheless continues to be an observant Jew, Berthold is at first at a loss for an answer, but finally it emerges that he has trust in his people and their religious traditions, and continues to obey the commandments of the Torah out of love for his people. In his mind love of the Jewish people includes *eo ipso* the traditions which have shaped them, and he, therefore, cannot conceive of the people detached from the religious traditions which have kept them alive through the ages. It is this "affective" faith, expressing itself in trust, fidelity, and constancy, which prevents Berthold from drawing logical conclusions from his doubts and misgivings. The Orthodox way of life, Breuer would appear to hold, need not be abandoned because of intellectual skepticism. On the contrary, religious conduct acts as a bulwark against defection until such time as inner uncertainties, typical of youths, are overcome by Jewish life itself. In the nocturnal scene referred to above, the Book of Psalms is quoted as a source of consolation for a heart stricken by the pangs of doubt.

How, it may be asked, does the adherence to Jewish religious life help to still skeptical notions arising in the intellectual sphere? Surely Breuer does not attribute it to custom solely, though custom, the basis for many facets of our life, is not without value in this connection. Faith and doubt being universal phenomena, we have it on the authority of the great religious genius Blaise Pascal that the three sources of religious belief are reason, custom, and inspiration, which ideally supplement and reinforce each other. Custom alone without conviction and inspiration may be an insufficient vehicle for the adoption and inculcation of religious faith. Yet it does play a role, particularly if supported by an "affective" inclination toward a people and admiration of its traditions. Religious inspiration, a rare phenomenon, is often aroused by participation in a communal act, such as worship or religious study, causing doubts of a doctrinal nature to recede, or vindicating by the sheer force of religious experience the principles of faith previously eroded by doubt.

Norman Lamm's essay on the subject of religious doubt, cited above, continues the trend of thought initiated by Breuer. Most of Lamm's ideas are to be found, albeit in germinal form, in Breuer's works. Lamm's essay, however, is marked by a clear conceptualization of the phenomena under discussion, and in view of the wealth of his sources and the lucidity displayed in their exposition, it represents the only systematic and comprehensive work written on the subject by an Orthodox Jewish author.

Lamm adopts Buber's distinction between "faith in," which characterizes Judaism, and "faith that," which is typical of Christianity. In actual fact, and contrary to Buber's submission, both types of faith are accepted in Judaism: the divine inspiration of Torah exemplifies "faith in," the first type of belief; that the children of Israel were slaves in Egypt and miraculously rescued from bondage represents the second type, "faith that." Lamm calls the first type "affective faith," because of the element of trust it involves, and the second type, which expresses assent to a set of metaphysical or axiological propositons (e.g., the belief in God as Creator of the Universe, man having been created in the image of God), he calls "cognitive faith." To these two categories of faith he adds a third, "functional faith," which is the behavioral form of trust in the rightness, justification, and binding force of Halakhah.

Three types of doubt correspond to these three types of faith, of which the most widespread in our time is the cognitive. In Lamm's own words,

> In an age of instant worldwide communication, where every stray remark of casual *apikorsut* is trumpeted forth throughout the world as a sensational discovery of revolutionary import, and when so many people are graduates of colleges where their instructors delight in shaking them loose from any religious convictions and moral moorings—in an age of this sort, simple, wholesome, unquestioning faith has largely vanished. When faith is come by today, it must struggle relentlessly in unending tension with doubt. So many faiths, both religious and secular, have proved disappointing, that many a thoughtful man is afraid to give himself wholeheartedly to anything, lest such dedication lead to more frustration and heartache.[7]

This is an acceptable analysis of a certain facet of the present-day intellectual climate. But in order to further substantiate and explain our present-day proneness and susceptibility to religious doubt, we should remember that it is not only the popular type of *apikorsut* trumpeted throughout the world that influences our generation. The skepticism and agnosticism prevalent in present-day universities represent the diluted and often distorted brand of the more serious kind of *apikorsut* which results from the philosophical views of the more creative and formative spirits of our time. These influence thoughtful minds, who in their turn inculcate their skepticism to a wider public. Whether we like it or not, we are exposed in varying degree to the theories and ideas of such philosophers as Jean-Paul Sartre, Bertrand Russell, Ludwig Wittgenstein, and Karl Popper, to mention just a few of them. It is, in other words, the *Zeitgeist* in its various manifestations, coupled with the technological means of disseminating knowledge and information on a scale unthought of in previous times, which makes the relentless struggle against religious doubt necessary, even in those who by nature or education are favorably inclined to religion.

The same point is emphasized with perception by the well-known Christian theologian Richard R. Niebuhr.

But clearly we cannot attribute all doubting to the limitedness of our understanding or to the deficiency of our being when it is the presence of other men in ourselves through our imagination and sympathy that give birth to so much of our doubting. Curiously or perversely we are enriched by such uncertainty. Therefore doubting is not simply a sign of weakness. It is rather one of the threads in the ever more complex web binding the individual into his generation. The prevalence of doubting attests to the pervasiveness with which the saeculum is present in the individual. Never has the individual been so much a conscious part of his age. Seldom has he felt himself so compelled to join its attacks on his own security.[8]

We see that Niebuhr, far from regarding religious doubt as a sign of weakness in religious conviction, appreciates its positive aspects, claiming that the uncertainty created by doubt enriches us in that it witnesses our relatedness to the minds of our contemporaries. It seems to me that this positive appreciation of doubt as an inevitable concomitant and even corrective of faith is a rather modern phenomenon, understandable in view of the prevalent intellectual climate and not confined to the religious outlook of Christian theologians. The American Orthodox rabbi Emanual Rackman says in terms similar to those of Niebuhr:

Perhaps, like Socrates, I corrupt youth, but I do teach that Judaism encourages questioning even as it enjoins faith and commitment. A Jew dare not live with absolute certainty, not only because certainty is the hallmark of the fanatic, and Judaism abhors fanaticism, but also because doubt is good for the human soul, its humility and consequently its greater potential ultimately to discover its creator.[9]

This indeed is a legitimate expression of modern Orthodoxy willing to preach openness of mind—"Torah coupled with general culture"—and therefore unable to shut out currents of thought critical of religion. However, the interesting point in Rackman's argument is the fact that he, like his Christian colleagues, does not regret this development but on the contrary welcomes it, because in his view doubt acts as a refining element of faith, fostering humility and precluding fanaticism.

The German-American theologian and philosopher Paul Tillich goes even further and regards doubt as a permanent element inherent in faith as such, and he adopts this stance from a structural, or, put in a different way, a phenomenological viewpoint.

Doubt is not a permanent experience within the act of faith, but it is always present as an element in the structure of faith. This is the difference between faith and immediate evidence either of perceptual or of logical character. There is no faith without an intrinsic "in spite of,"[10] and the courageous affirmation of oneself in the state of ultimate concern. . . . If doubt appears, it should not be considered as the negation of faith, but as an element which was always and will always be present in the act of faith. Existential doubt and faith are poles of the same reality, the state of ultimate concern.[11]

We note by implication the distinction Tillich makes between simple and existential faith. Simple faith is possible without doubt, a fact supported by considerable evidence of which the theologian Tillich was certainly aware. There is, of course, naive and unreflecting faith, not subject to erosion by doubt at all, but what Tillich calls existential faith is a far more complex phenomenon. It is one thing to say that religious doubt is the result of the presence of other minds in our own, or put differently, evidence of the penetration of the *Zeitgeist* into the recesses of our minds and souls; it is another thing to claim—as Tillich does—that doubt is structurally anchored in religious faith, forming, as it were, a constitutive characteristic thereof, in contradistinction to facts of a perceptual or logical nature.

If I were asked to point out an analogous conception of religious faith by an Orthodox Jewish writer, I would refer to the article "Al ha-Safek" by a veteran Israeli educator, composed of a series of letters in which a young teacher discusses the subject of religious doubt with an older and more experienced colleague.[12]

At the end of the article the author sums up his argument: "All pragmatic arguments aimed at bypassing religious doubt are simply unfounded and unjustified. Doubt and religious faith descended from heaven bound together. Doubt without faith leads to nihilism; faith without doubt to fanaticism." He then offers the following advice to the reader: "Cast doubt upon the unessential, and believe in that which is essential. What is essential and what is unessential is something that every person must decide for himself."[13] This last sentence appears somewhat sweeping in its permissive intent, coming as it does from the pen of an Orthodox writer. The distinction between essential and nonessential belief may be valid in itself, but allocation to one or the other category cannot rest entirely on personal feeling, taste, or choice. To illustrate this point, let us consider two examples of Jewish traditional belief. In the daily prayer book we refer to God as *Adon Olam* ("Lord of the Universe"), with all the implications of such an appellation; there is also a prayer for the welfare of the State of Israel which marks "the first budding forth of our redemption." Surely these two affirmations, both incorporated in the statutory prayer book, are not of the same status. It may be legitimate to regard the second affirmation as inessential, especially if viewed through non-Zionist eyes, and to cast doubt upon its religious validity. On the other hand, seen with Orthodox eyes, the individual is not in a position to choose the second affirmation and cast doubt upon the first. But to revert to the main argument: the Jewish counterpart of Paul Tillich's conception of faith and doubt is to be found in the first sentence of our quotation, namely, that faith and doubt are phenomena inseparably linked together ("having descended from heaven bound together") and, I should now like to add, not entirely dependent on the intellectual climate of a particular era.

The idea of the omnipresence of doubt in religious faith is found in Hassidic thought, particularly of the Bratslaver kind.

Arthur Green's biography of Rabbi Nachman makes it clear that even a man of religious genius like the saintly Rabbi Nachman is more often than not tormented by religious doubt, the feeling that God is absent from His world despite repeated efforts at meditation and prayer. According to Green: "Man lives in a world where God cannot be seen; given this reality, doubt is an inevitable part of the life of every religious human being and the denial of God's very existence is something at which the faithful cannot afford to scoff."[14]

This indeed is merely another formulation of Tillich's conception of existential doubt, a term also used by Mordecai Cohen, with the difference that it is expressed here with greater assuredness and intensity. Moreover, on reading Green's biography one gains the impression that Rabbi Nachman's conception of faith and doubt is a far more complex and intricate phenomenon than that presented by the other religious thinkers referred to here; for according to Rabbi Nachman, as interpreted by Green, religious faith and doubt, or "challenge" (*maqqif*, because it inextricably "surrounds" or "envelops" the mind), represent a constant challenge to faith. According to Green:

> As a person sets out on his search for God he is confronted by a seemingly endless series of such *maqqifim*; as each doubt or challenge that stands before him is resolved, another comes to takes its place. The path to knowledge of God is one of spiralling ascent, each step of the way marked by successively more difficult challenges to face.[15]

Two points require to be dealt with. Green speaks of knowledge of God, but what he means is religious faith in a more general sense. The most outstanding and prominent tenet of that faith is, of course, belief in God, or to be more precise, the existential certainty of His presence, and our ability to be aware of it and render service to Him. The second point refers to the interesting concept of the "spiralling ascent," which, metaphorically speaking, expresses the notion of faith as a phenomenon growing and developing in gradual stages, while constantly being fostered by doubt or challenge, which paradoxically is experienced as absence of God. To put this paradox more succinctly: one has to be plagued by the tormenting feeling of God's absence from one's life in order to experience true faith in Him and His presence.

The dialectical nature of faith, involving constant wrestling with challenges, must be viewed in contradistinction to simple faith with its assuredness of God's presence. The first characterizes the *Zaddiq*, the tormented master, the second the ordinary believers, who need reassurance in their own simple faith, without being imbued with the tormented struggles of their religious models. The complexity of such a situation makes it understandable that ultimately the religious master, too, experiences a strong yearning for simple faith. Here again, is Green's comment:

> The polemical nature of Nachman's faith-idea has caused him to come full circle back to the idealization of simplicity. Reason, to Nachman, is the great enemy of religious faith. It is only by fighting the claims of reason and ultimately by transcending the rational mind itself that true faith can come to be. God is completely beyond the ken of any intellectuality; beyond even such wisdom as is properly permitted within the bounds of Torah. The greatest faith has no basis in intellect, and cannot be proven in any way.[16]

From this passage we learn that Rabbi Nachman's "challenges" are not to be viewed as mystical entities—in the nature of the "angels of evil" or *masṭinim* referred to in some of our prayers—and that the doubts "enveloping" faith stem from purely rational considerations. This takes us back again to simple faith, which Nachman viewed as the ideal. When trying to sum up the various characteristics of Nachman's faith there emerges an image of

such considerable complexity that it appears to contain something of everything. It is dialectical and yet aims at simplicity, it is
existential and yet mystical, as Green shows toward the end of his
chapter on the subject. It includes doubt as an almost necessary
precondition and yet aims at dispelling it, regarding simple faith
as the ideal. The phenomenon may, however, appear less confus-
ing if we view faith as a growing manifestation passing through a
series of stages, and because of its individual character dependent on a great variety of psychological factors. In any case it is
not my aim to unravel the mysteries of this problem, even if it
were possible. Suffice it to state—and this, I hope, has been amply
demonstrated—that religious doubt plays a prominent role in
Rabbi Nachman's thought.

To come back to Lamm's categorization of faith and doubt:
What he calls "affective" faith springs from love of God, trust and
reliance in Him, and the category of doubt corresponding to this
type of faith is already legitimized in the Bible because it is a
concomitant of man's relation to God. It may even be argued that
the closer and more intimate this relationship, the more intensive
the human reaction to the injustices, cruelties, and catastrophes
experienced in a world controlled by Divine Providence. We find
Abraham arguing with God and asking Him rather reproachfully,
"Wilt Thou consume the righteous with the wicked?" (Genesis
18:23).

We note Jeremiah's outcry: "Wherefore does the way of the
wicked prosper? Wherefore are all those happy that deal very
treacherously?" (Jeremiah 12:1); similarly Job: "It is all one.
Therefore I say that He destroys the innocent with the wicked"
(Job 9:22) and the prophet Habakkuk: "Wherefore lookest Thou
upon them that deal treacherously and holdest Thy tongue when
the wicked devoureth the man that is more righteous than he?"
(Habakkuk 2:12). The tragic events of the Holocaust are an
immensely intensified parallel to the previously quoted biblical
instances of the question *Unde malum?*—"Whence cometh the
evil?"—that looms so large in the lives of believers as well as
nonbelievers. Viewed theologically, i.e., from the point of view of
our tentative knowledge of the divinity and its attributes as
revealed in the Bible, the events of the Holocaust do not represent
substantially novel phenomena. Let me quote Eliezer Berkovits:

When one questions the act of an absolute God whose every attribute, too, is absolute by definition, the suffering of a single innocent person is as incomprehensible as that of milions, not because the suffering of millions matters as little as those of one human being, but because with Him the suffering of the one ought to be as scandalous as that of multitudes.[17]

Here, we are dealing with the perennial problem of theodicy, the unprecedented dimensions of evil that threaten to engulf and extinguish the faith of the believer. The conventional theological answers to this ancient problem (the Lord's ways are not our ways; the secret things belong to the Lord; the Deity is hiding His face, withdrawing, as it were, from the human world; the Lurian idea of *zimzum*, a self-imposed limitation and diminution of His dominion, etc.), all these offer cold comfort to those who have experienced the horrors of the Holocaust. Those survivors whose faith has remained unimpaired in spite of such tribulations and traumatic experiences truly deserve to inspire our admiration.

Neither the plausibility nor the legitimacy of religious doubt can be questioned, as the evidence I have gathered from the writings of a variety of religious thinkers shows. The Jewish philosophers I have dealt with so far belong to the Orthodox stream, but those of other schools have also contributed to the problem under discussion. Since the point argued in this chapter is the legitimacy of religious doubt within the confines of traditional Judaism I have had to limit myself to the views of avowedly Orthodox religious writers.

To sum up, the various conceptions of religious doubt, as we have seen, refer in the majority of instances to what has been called "cognitive" doubt. This has been viewed as mainly a young people's problem (Isaac Breuer), a symptom of insufficient maturity stemming to a large extent from inadequate study and lack of religious knowledge and experience. Or it is viewed as a phenomenon not necessarily connected with a certain stage of intellectual development, but rather a consequence of and the price exacted for the openness of the *Torah im derekh erez* type of traditional Judaism. In this case ideas from a nonreligious intellectual background are absorbed and clash with traditional Jewish conceptions. Or the view has been taken that religious doubt is, struc-

turally speaking, an integral part of religious faith because of the
specific nature of religious truth, which is fundamentally different from scientific truth. Here, however, I would interpolate a few
critical coments. The very word *emunah* implies firmness, reliability, trust, which actually excludes the notion of doubt. It is
therefore only natural that a man of the religious stature of Chief
Rabbi Avraham Yitzhak Hacohen Kook speaks of "the integrity of
faith which is firmly embedded in our innermost selves."[18] It
appears to me that the notion of faith as necessarily accompanied
and hence threatened by doubt does not characterize the "perfect
believer"—the one who believes *be'emunah shelemah*. We may
regard as an exception the Hassidic conception of the Bratslaver
brand, which actually welcomes "challenges" and doubts as factors leading to the purification and elevation of faith to ever
higher levels of spirituality, though at the same time extolling the
ideal of simple faith.

All the writers quoted in this chapter agree about the whole-
someness of simple faith which is not consciously shaken by
outside influences. They also agree that the existence of religious
doubt should by no means lead to actual contravention of religious laws. In other words, the obligation to fulfill Torah commandments remains intact and independent of psychological
exigencies. Moreover, some of the writers mentioned in this
chapter stress the intellectual freedom of the Orthodox Jew as
being supported by and anchored in his unswerving loyalty and
commitment to the Torah.

6

Torah min Ha-Shamayim in Neo-Orthodox Perspective

As a Kantian philosopher, Isaac Breuer incorporated Kant's epistomological stance, in particular his fundamental distinction between phenomena and noumena, the world as appearance and the world as it is (*an-sich*), in his own philosophy. He uses this Kantian distinction skillfully in order to neutralize the danger to Orthodoxy lurking in theories of higher biblical criticism. He does not see the need to enter into detailed polemics with these critics of the Bible, because, to use his nomenclature, they refer to the biblical text as "phenomenon" without taking cognizance of the Bible as "noumenon." In other words, they act upon the assumption that the Bible is a genre of literature of admittedly high caliber but of human origin. Hence it is capable of being examined, like other creations of the human mind, by accepted literary criteria relating to composition, style, imagery, vocabulary, and any other method used in literary research. Breuer claims that the findings of such research bear no relevance to the Torah as "noumenon," since it is not open to conventional means of literary investigation. Those Bible scholars who regard its written text as the sole subject of inquiry, according to Breuer, remain involved in the superficial verbal clothing of Torah, without penetrating its depth—the hidden mysteries which are its very soul and innermost core, whose explication is entrusted to the true believers among the Jewish people.

It might be asked what faithful Jewish believers know about the Torah as "noumenon" if, according to Kant-Breuer, "noumenon" stands for the eternally unknown X which human intelligence can never reach out to grasp. Breuer's answer is that the Oral Torah represents the instrument by means of which the Almighty has made it possible for His faithful flock to unravel as much of the Torah *an-sich* as was necessary to shape His people's lives, their history and destiny. However, he goes on to claim that even the Oral Torah does not represent the exhaustive sum total of its ultimate content. "Even if with the help of oral tradition we acquire the understanding of a portion of the Torah *an sich*— even then, the latter still continues to abide in its linkage to the Godhead in immaculate objectivity."[1]

It is quite clear that Breuer's ideas about *Torah min ha-sha-mayim*, which are laden with mystic allusions, in effect represent a peculiar fusion of Kant's epistomology and ideas borrowed from Kabbalah, particularly the branch of it that he acquired from the study of *The Two Tablets of Stone* by Rabbi Isaiah Horowitz (1550–1625). His philosophic stance at this stage may be summed up as follows: The written text merely represents the outer garb, hiding its true meaning from the reader. It has to be read with the help of the fundamental hermeneutic rules and other interpretations of the oral tradition. However, even when this procedure is followed, the Torah as "noumenon" continues to be veiled in mystery. The truth of the Written Torah is vouchsafed by the Oral Torah, and that of the Oral Torah by *Knesset Yisrael*— a mystically charged concept—which stands for the people of Israel in their linkage to the Godhead. The underlying conception may be characterized as the mysterious triple identity of the Godhead with *Knesset Yisrael* and Torah. This constitutes an important tenet of Kabbalah, quoted frequently as if originally expounded in the *Zohar*, though it is in fact not clearly spelled out in this work.[2]

To spell out more clearly Breuer's basic assumptions: Written Torah yields something of its innermost kernel if interpreted and accepted in the light of the Oral Torah, most of whose interpretations and conclusions bear a normative character demanding total commitment on the part of the believer. In addition, the written text of the Torah admits a secret mystical interpretation accessible only to those initiated into its esoteric lore. Finally, all these presuppositions are placed by Breuer into a framework of Kantian epistemology with its fundamental distinction between "phenomena" and "noumena."

Once these assumptions are accepted, all the elaborations of modern Bible criticism become irrelevant, since modern biblical scholarship is based on entirely different presuppositions from Breuer's. The modern biblical scholar engages solely in the literary interpretation of the written text, and he regards its mystical undercurrents as a metaphysical accretion. For Breuer higher criticism is so irrelevant to his way of thinking that he considers it completely unnecessary to engage in polemics to disprove its conclusions. However, the attempt to discredit higher criticism on its own assumptions was made in Breuer's day by some Orthodox scholars, the most notable among whom was Rabbi David Z'vi Hoffmann of the Berlin Hildesheimer Seminary. This eminent scholar undertook the arduous task of examining the methodological procedures, theories, and conclusions of the propounders of higher criticism and other related schools of biblical scholarship, with the aim of disproving them or at least of calling them into question, if they contradicted accepted religious notions of traditional Judaism. Rabbi Hoffmann did all this by wrestling with his opponents in a common arena, attacking their linguistic, historical, and archaeological assumptions and conclusions on purely scientific grounds.

The rather involved argumentation of Isaac Breuer relating to higher criticism was simplified some forty years later by his nephew, Rabbi Mordecai Breuer, who, though accepting the main theses of his learned uncle on the theme of Torah min hashamayim, gave the argument an interesting twist. His two essays on this subject, essentially a variation on his uncle's basic thesis, were published in the Jerusalem journal Deot.[3] They were followed by a discussion with a number of Jerusalem scholars, some of them Orthodox. It is interesting to note that none of these scholars agreed with him.

Mordecai Breuer's line of argument may be seen as a simplified version of his late uncle's more lengthy and involved discourses from which the Kantian epistemological basis fundamental to the uncle's theories has been eliminated. This may be regarded as a step in the right direction for two reasons.

1. When arguing a case or trying to solve a problem, it is advisable to reduce preconceptions to a minimum. It might be argued that the Kantian epistemological stance is dispensable even to Isaac Breuer's train of thought, which could have rested solely on the two remaining religious factors: faith in the binding character of the Oral Law and acceptance of the kabbalistic interpretation of Torah as revelation of its innermost core. Hence it is not surprising that Mordecai Breuer made no use of Kantian epistemology; in fact there is a total absence of Kantian influence in his writings.

2. The Kantian distinction between "phenomena" and "noumena," and the illustrious philosopher's belief in the mysterious *Ding an-sich,* inaccessible to human intelligence, is no longer acceptable to modern epistemological thought. Thus Mordecai Breuer rightly refrained from burdening his argument with a presupposition which has become obsolescent.

However, the elimination of Kantian influence from Mordecai Breuer's thought does not constitute the only point of difference between his and his uncle's positions. His essays reveal a much more positive appreciation of modern biblical criticism than his learned uncle was prepared to concede, and he argues that scholarship, biblical or other, is a function of *hokhmah,* which is not only the prerogative of Israel, but manifest also to the same degree in the gentile world. Hence it is not surprising that the gentile contribution to the investigation of the Bible is so impressive and deserving of serious consideration. This prima facie judgment is confirmed and reinforced by Mordecai Breuer's serious study of the craftsmanship of the higher criticism of the Graf-Wellhausen school as well as of other modern biblical scholars. He is impressed by their sifting of biblical text according to source material based on the nature of the divine names occurring in them, and he seriously ponders the Wellhausen school's conclusion relating to the non-Mosaic, much later origin of the Scriptures (at the earliest during or after the kingdom of David, about 1000 B.C.E., some parts even later). In short, he reaches the conclusion that the scientific exegesis of the Bible represents a serious scholarly discipline. He even goes so far as to regard its conclusions as unassailable, provided one remembers that these scholars relate to the Bible as a human document and that their methodology is consistent with accepted ways of exploring and analyzing other literary creations.

Mordecai Breuer would argue that if we view the Torah from the standpoint of its outward garb, we are bound to conclude that it represents a complex and ingeniously structured edifice composed of many layers based on a variety of sources. We may detect in it contradictions, changes of style, explanatory notes, and other addenda contributed by editors. If, however, we endeavor to extract from the Torah its secret, esoteric kernel by making use of kabbalistic interpretations, the picture we get changes radically, so much so that the observations of higher criticism, reflecting its heterogeneous and highly complex structure, are no longer relevant. The two different ways of viewing the Torah resemble observations relating to two entirely different objects.

Once one adopts Mordecai Breuer's approach and follows his argument, one can easily understand the parallel he draws between the Torah and human life in general. Are there not contradictions, enigmas, and mysteries in human life at large, in world history, and in our natural surroundings? And did not the Almighty envision the Torah and create the universe according to the Torah's blueprint? Why then should we expect to fathom the mysteries of the Torah more than those of the universe?

This recourse to Kabbalah is obviously intended to rescue belief in *Torah min ha-shamayim* in its traditional interpretation from the eroding influence of higher criticism. However, Breuer's motivation seems to be more complex. He claims that the scientific research of the Bible has lost impetus and in fact exhausted itself. He believes that no further striking discoveries will be forthcoming, just as we do not expect completely novel revelations concerning the works of Shakespeare, Goethe, and other classical poets. The alleged stagnation of scientific Bible scholarship seems to encourage his turning to mystical homilies which he finds more

interesting and satisfactory. But it is also possible that this
turning away from rational thought is somehow part of the
current vogue of mysticism and that "diminished confidence in
our mind," the feeling that rational thought has become discred-
ited, which has been diagnosed as typical of our time by literary
scholars.[4]

There is another point of difference between the attitudes of the
two Breuers. Mordecai Breuer's essays reveal the deep influence of
Rabbi Avraham Isaac Hacohen Kook, absent in the writings of the
elder Breuer. It is mainly the idea of *kiddush ha-hilloniut*—the
sanctification of the secular and worldly—so central in Rabbi
Kook's thought, that influenced Mordecai Breuer. This sanctification is made possible by what may be called a dialectical process.
To quote Rabbi Kook in a somewhat free translation:

> Views and thinking processes affected by *minut*, i.e., heresy,
> ideas incompatible with a traditional Jewish outlook, once they
> are analyzed and their roots disclosed, lead by virtue of their
> very nature to deeper and loftier religious faith—more alive and
> more illuminating than the simple, unquestioning religious
> belief prevailing before the breach became manifest.[5]

Here is a further explanatory passage from Rabbi Kook's writings also quoted by Mordecai Breuer:

> It is a great and important principle in the war of ideas that if
> an opinion is asserted which tends to contradict and refute any
> idea of Torah, we need not at the outset attempt to disprove and
> reject it, but rather endeavor to superimpose the castle of
> Torah, and thereby we become elevated, and in the process the
> ideas become revealed in their clarity; then we are no longer
> oppressed by anything. So we may, with a heart full of confi-
> dence, confront these ideas afresh.[6]

We may be asking too much of a philosopher of mysticism if we
expect him to spell out his ideas with perfect lucidity. However, if
we try to interpret the metaphors used in these quotations and
attune ourselves to their style, then the general tenor of the

quoted passages becomes clear, and we also understand the use Mordecai Breuer makes of the ideas embodied in them. The message he tries to get across to us is that instead of opposing academic Bible exegesis, we had better try to accommodate it within our own religious system. This may be done, in the first place, by admitting that many of the problems dealt with by higher criticism have already been raised and differently solved by the rabbis of old as well as by modern traditionalist Jewish Bible commentators. Moreover, having done this, we may now "superimpose upon it the castle of Torah" by relegating the findings of higher criticism to the outward shell of Torah, which leaves its innermost kernel entirely unaffected by it.

As already pointed out, Mordecai Breuer supports his reliance on Kabbalah by claiming that nontraditional Bible research has already spent its energies and is merely rehashing, mitigating, and modifying the findings of the Wellhausen school. He does not expect any resounding discoveries concerning the Bible to be forthcoming, just as literary scholars no longer expect revolutionary disclosures concerning the work of the classical poets. The research into all these—the Bible as well as the literary classics—may be regarded as virtually complete. In the case of the Bible, this makes the recourse to kabbalistic conceptions not only understandable but most welcome.

Professor Z. R. Werblowsky of the Hebrew University draws attention to a further point which, although it may easily be overlooked by the reader of Mordecai Breuer's essays, brings out very strongly how far he leaned on Rabbi Kook's ideas.[7] It should be remembered that Rabbi Kook firmly believed in the messianic inauguration of his time, a conviction he cautiously clothed in his writings in kabbalistic metaphors. In such times, when the revelation of the ways of the Almighty and their hidden purport is awaited, the special temptation in the form of heresy and even idolatry should be viewed as a provocation and challenge to be overcome in order to make known with greater force faith in the oneness of God and His name. Paradoxically speaking, the messianic era, more than any other, is capable of elevating profaneness to the level of sanctity.

Moreover, Werblowsky tries to explain Mordecai Breuer's somewhat exaggerated praise of the Wellhausen school, which the latter represents as an example of biblical scholarship par excellence in spite of the fact that some of its assumptions and hypotheses have in the meantime been abandoned by a number of erudite Bible scholars.[8]

Werblowsky regards the affinity between the Orthodox Breuer and the Wellhausen school—paradoxical as it may appear—more as a symbol than a real token of intellectual affiliation. It expresses the idea that even a radically critical school such as Wellhausen's, with its destructive approach to Orthodox religious faith, may be sublimated and utilized in order to illuminate the inner significance of Torah meaning and thus divested of its negative import. But how is this "elevation" brought about? Werblowsky explains:

> The *peshat* [plain meaning] as revealed by higher criticism points to the kabbalistic interpretation at least inasmuch as it discloses the external structures [of the text] whose inward content is the subject of mystic lore. Fundamentally, the *peshat* points to the kabbalistic interpretation, which in turn is not understandable in its inherent intention without the critical *peshat*. The latter appears transparent to the believer inasmuch as it enables him to penetrate the outer shell of Scripture and to reach its inner kernel. Thus Wellhausen's theories, which [to the Orthodox] appear to be conceived from impure motives, were fashioned by Mordecai Breuer into a key that helps to open up the mysteries of Torah.[9]

But it may still be asked whether this radical recourse to Kabbalah is, in the final analysis, really capable of sustaining the Mosaic authorship of the Bible. For this precisely is the crucial point in the conflict between the traditional belief of Orthodoxy and higher criticism. Professor Jacob Katz of the Hebrew University adroitly pointed out, during the discussion following the publication of Mordecai Breuer's articles, that it is precisely the *historical* method, as applied to biblical research, which has engendered the conflict with the Orthodox doctrine of *Torah min ha-shamayim*, as expounded in the Talmud and adopted by

Maimonides and other traditional philosophers up to and including Isaac Breuer. It cannot be denied that the same historical method that raised problems in relation to Bible research may raise the same—if not more severe—difficulties in relation to research into Kabbalah. To put the problem in a nutshell: It might be asked whether the Mosaic authorship of the Bible is capable of being sustained by a religious school of thought of very late origin. In this context I should like to quote a definition of Kabbalah by the late Gershom Scholem.

> Kabbalah, it must be remembered, is not the name of a certain dogma or system, but rather the general term applied to a whole religious movement. This movement, with some of whose stages and tendencies we shall have to acquaint ourselves, has been going on from Talmudic times to the present day. Its development has been uninterrupted, though by no means uniform and often dramatic. It leads from Rabbi Akiva of whom the Talmud says that he left the "Paradise" of mystical speculation safe and sane as he had entered it—something that indeed cannot be said of every Kabbalist—to the late Rabbi Avraham Isaac Kook, the leader of the Jewish community in Palestine and a splendid type of Jewish mystic.[10]

If Scholem is right in his assertion that the kabbalistic movement was initiated as late as talmudic times, the attempt to sustain the belief in the Mosaic authorship of Torah by deflecting our viewpoint from the ordinary *peshat* to its kabbalistic interpretation can, methodologically speaking, hardly be considered conclusive. On the other hand, can it really be claimed with fair certainty that Kabbalah is a religious movement originating with Rabbi Akiba's entry into the "Garden," as reported in the Talmud (*Hagigah* 14b), together with Ben-Azzai, Ben-Zoma, and Aḥer? Is it not at least possible, if not likely, that there were earlier traditions of mystical lore, just as the Mishnah, though finally edited about 200 c.e., goes back to much earlier traditions, as set out in the *Ethics of the Fathers* in genealogical fashion, and further elaborated in detail by Maimonides in the introduction to his Commentary to the Mishnah?

I have already drawn attention to the fact that Mordecai Breuer argues his point by means of manipulating a smaller number of preconceptions than his learned uncle did. However, there is a further reduction of preconceived elements in the religious thought of Yeshayahu Leibowitz relevant to the problem under discussion.

Thus, we witness that the number of preconceptions applied by the above-mentioned scholars in their wrestling with the problem of *Torah min ha-shamayim* is on a descending scale. The corollary of this observation is reflected in the gradual unraveling of the problem which, handled by Leibowitz, boils down to a rather simple solution.

The fact that Leibowitz is primarily a scientist would explain why he makes no use of mystical explanations of the text of the Torah. When presenting his own solution to the problem—Orthodoxy versus scientific Bible research and science in general—the only concepts he uses are the written text of the Torah and its divinely inspired interpretation embodied in the Oral Law. When comparing the two, the Written and the Oral Law, Leibowitz stresses the subordination of the former to the latter, because it was the sages themselves who determined the composition of the biblical canon and authoritatively fixed its interpretation. According to Leibowitz, the results of higher criticism are irrelevant to the Orthodox believer who accepts the Oral Law as the only competent guide to the Scriptures. Hence we might say that *Torah min ha-shamayim* is interpreted by Leibowitz as rooted in *emunat hakhamim,* i.e., acceptance of the authoritative status of the sages, whose interpretations and religious rulings demand total commitment. Leibowitz would certainly agree that it is at the express behest of the Written Torah that the rabbis be regarded as its authoritative interpreters, as we read in Deuteronomy 17:11.

According to the tenor of the law which they shall teach thee, and according to the judgment which they shall tell thee, thou shalt do. Thou shalt not turn aside from the sentence which they shall show thee to the right hand or to the left.

Let us hear Leibowitz himself on this point.

The fact that the Bible as such was accepted by a large sector of mankind did not make it a Jewish book. That means to say that the Bible in itself represents no constitutive element of Judaism—in contrast to the prayer book and to Halakhah, which of course are. Historic Judaism is not based on the Written Torah but on the Oral one, and it will not survive unless the Oral Law becomes a living reality and is not itself turned into Written Torah. To view the Bible as it is (without the Oral Law) as the Book of Books, and use it in this sense as an educational factor in a general humanistic framework, is merely the outcome of a narrow, nationalistic chauvinism.[11]

Indeed, if we view Judaism as the scientist Leibowitz does, as a historico-empirical phenomenon, we cannot but admit that it is characterized by Halakhah, and that the Jewish way of life is molded by observance of religious commandments. Once this empirical fact is accepted as the core of Judaism, the various theories of scientific Bible research need not unduly worry the observant Jew. What matters is *kiyum mitzvot* ("to keep the commandments")—and this cannot be undermined or disproved by theories about the composition of the Written Torah, which in any case is only subordinate to its halakhic interpretations. The results of scientific research may indeed contradict factual statements in the Bible, but not religious commandments. This is a logical truth, says Professor Gershom Weiler in a perceptive article on Yeshayahu Leibowitz's Jewish philosophy.[12]

What these three scholars have in common is the theologian's deep concern for the validity of the doctrinal basis of traditional Judaism and the determination to defend it against possible inroads by a secular scholarly discipline. Whereas the two Breuers fall back on Kabbalah, which they consider safe from the erosion wrought by biblical research, Leibowitz emphasizes the subordinate status of the written text of Torah to the Oral Law. Thus he takes refuge in the Oral Law, which he considers a dynamic force, vital and developing throughout the generations. On the other hand, there is Rabbi David Z'vi Hoffmann's attempt to defend the traditional concept of *Torah min ha-shamayim* on scholarly exegetic grounds. To this category of Bible scholars belongs the late Chief Rabbi of Great Britain, Dr. Joseph Herman Hertz, who used a more popular approach and a rather eclectic method in his commentary to the Pentateuch.[13]

In light of the problems raised by these philosophers, traditional Judaism might be expected to stress such ideas inherent in rabbinical literature as interpret the concept of *Torah min hashamayim* rather flexibly. Such a reaction would make use of the view expressed in the Talmud that the Torah was transmitted in separate scrolls (*megilot, megilot*) at different times and occasions, both before and after the Sinaitic Covenant (*Gittin* 60a). Thus we read for instance in Exodus 15:25, "There [in Marah] He made for them a statute and an ordinance, and there He proved them." According to the Talmud (*Sanhedrin* 65b) what is meant are social laws, the Sabbath, and honoring one's parents, which already then had been given to the Israelites. Thus, the instruction of the people preceded and followed the Sinaitic Covenant throughout the years of wandering in the wilderness. We can gain a vivid insight into the tremendous development of the Oral Law throughout the generations if we reflect upon the story reported in the Talmud (*Menachot* 29b) where Moses is miraculously transported to the Academy of Rabbi Akiva and surprisingly enough, or rather understandably, was unable to follow the halakhic discourse conducted there. "He sat at the end of the eighteen rows of disciples and did not know what they were saying. He was overcome by faintness until one of the students asked . . . Rabbi Akiva, 'How do you know this or that thing? . . . ' The latter replied, 'It is *Halakhah le-Moshe mi-Sinai*'; whereupon Moses recovered from his faintness."

This interesting story may be elucidated by way of analogy: We may very well understand all the logical axiomata of mathematics and yet be unable to grasp the very complicated manipulations, combinations, and deductions following from these axiomata evolved by successive generations of gifted mathematicians. It is in harmony with this idea of the immanent growth of the Oral Law that Rabbi Yehoshua ben Levi (first generation of Palestinian amoraim) makes the following comment on Exodus 34:27: "And the Lord said unto Moses, Write thou these words, for after the tenor of these words I have made a covenant with thee and with Israel." " 'The tenor of these words' includes Mikra, Mishnah,

Talmud, and Aggadah; even what an astute student [*talmid vatik*] will in future remark to his master has already been said to Moses on Sinai" (Jerusalem Talmud, *Peah* 2:4). It is obvious that the reference to the Sinaitic origin of the offshoots of the Oral Law is used here in a metaphoric sense, characterizing as it does the Torah in its immanent development throughout the ages. It follows that traditional Judaism is incompatible with fundamentalism, and that the written text of Torah in conjunction with its oral interpretation may be represented as the Tree of Life sprung from a seed which has blossomed, spreading out its ever-growing branches for eternity.

7

Universalism in the Philosophy of Rabbi Joseph B. Soloveitchik

Although Rabbi Joseph B. Soloveitchik's writings, particularly his essay "The Lonely Man of Faith," are well known to Jewish readers of English, I venture to offer further comment upon his work because I feel that an important aspect of his thought has not received the attention that it deserves.

Let me begin with "The Lonely Man of Faith." At the starting point of this essay are the two accounts of the creation of man in Genesis. Rabbi Soloveitchik points out four discrepancies in the two accounts, the most essential being the two different mandates given by God concerning the tasks which man was to fulfill in his earthly life. In focusing his attention on this point the author constructs a rich and elaborate web of reflections, which may be characterized as a philosophical homily of great originality and intellectual acumen.

To turn to the difference in mandates: Adam the First—the Adam whose creation is mentioned in the first chapter of Genesis—is told by the Almighty "to be fruitful and multiply, to fill the earth and subdue it." Adam the Second—so-called because of the account of the creation of man occurring in the second chapter—is commanded "to cultivate the Garden of Eden and keep it." There is no need to summarize the author's extremely elaborate description of Adam the First. Suffice it to quote one of the most salient statements about him:

Adam the First is overwhelmed by one quest: namely to harness and dominate the elemental natural forces and to put them at his disposal. This practical interest arouses his will to learn the secrets of nature. He is completely utilitarian as far as motivation, teleological design and methodology are concerned.

And there is another quotation in the same vein:

God in imparting the blessing to Adam the First and giving him the mandate to subdue nature, directed Adam's attention to the functional and practical aspects of his intellect through which Man is able to gain control over nature. Other intellectual inquiries, such as the metaphysical or axiologico-qualitative, no matter how incisive and penetrating, have never granted man dominion over his environment.[1]

To these attributes of Adam the author adds further characteristics drawn from the Psalms—especially Psalm 8—as well as various substantiations from talmudic and halakhic sources sometimes referred to in footnotes. These features, drawn from a variety of Jewish sources, are put together with considerable imaginative power. Thus, Rabbi Soloveitchik succeeds in presenting a portrait of the two types of man with a wealth of color which contrasts with the terse references to Adam in Genesis, the starting point of his reflections.

In Psalm 8 the eloquent proclamation of the unique stature of man is applied by the author to Adam the First: "for Thou hast made him a little lower than the angels and hast crowned him with glory and honor. . . . Thou madest him to have dominion over the works of Thy hand. Thou hast put all things under his feet." If we consider the content and implication of these two verses, we may readily accept the rabbi's assumption that they elaborate on the significant characteristics of Adam the First, who, according to the account in Genesis 1, was commanded to subdue the earth.

Moreover, the psalm brings out clealy man's dignity and glory, which are rooted in his ability to make his environment subservient to his purposes. However, the rabbi argues that there is no dignity without responsibility.

One cannot assume responsibility as long as one is incapable of living up to one's commitments. Only when Man rises to the heights of freedom of action and creativity of mind does he begin to implement the mandate of dignified responsibility entrusted to him by his Maker.[2]

We learn that Adam the First is not just a ruthless conqueror of the earth, driven by an overwhelming urge to assert himself and excel in his striving for power. His quest "to harness and dominate the elemental natural forces and to put them at his disposal" is tempered by a deeply ingrained sense of responsibility. In other words, there is a strong moral element inherent in his nature which enables him to control his aggressive striving for success. He is also endowed with the ability to create a community and translate ethical principles into legal norms, because a dignified existence is, of necessity, an orderly one, intolerant of lawlessness and anarchy. The author also attributes an aesthetic sense to Adam the First, calling him a creative aesthete whether engaged in an intellectual or artistic performance.

Just as there are halakhot which, in the words of the sages have little scriptural support, a fact that causes them "to hover in the air," so we may regard these aesthetic attributes of Adam the First. In justice to the author, it should be added that he substantiates this idea of an aesthetic attribute by reference to Maimonides' interpretation of the phrase "the tree of knowledge of good and evil" as the experience of pleasant and unpleasant emotions. However, the author seems to go beyond Maimonides' somewhat forced interpretation, since he explicitly states that Adam the First's conscience is energized not by the good but by the beautiful, a conception of ethics based entirely on aesthetics.

Rabbi Soloveitchik legitimizes even the intense urge of man to venture into the open spaces of a boundless universe, no matter how hazardous and fantastic these ventures may be. In his own words: "Man reaching for the distant stars is acting in harmony with his nature, which was created, willed and directed by his Maker."[3] This is rather surprising in view of the fact that God's original mandate to man was to subdue the earth and not the universe. According to the Book of Psalms, "the heavens are the

Lord's, and the earth He gave to man." At first sight, this would seem to set definite limits to man's aspirations.

According to Rabbi Soloveitchik, then, Adam the First is active, bold, and desirous of succeeding in the conquest of his environment. He is endowed with dignity and majesty. He is responsible and moral, his morality being rooted in his aesthetic sense. In the quest for knowledge he is pragmatic. This portrait tallies with the tacit assumption in Judaism, reflected in a wealth of rabbinic sources, that considers Adam to be as perfect as a human being can be because he was created by God Almighty and not begotten by man.

Adam the Second, it will be recalled, is commanded to cultivate and keep the Garden of Eden. In considering the edifice which, by means of deduction, the author erects on the basis of these few words, I am tempted to believe that he was aided by what may be called the associative method—frequently used in Jewish homiletical literature—though he himself does not expressly say so. *Avodah* suggests *avodat Hashem*, while *shemirah* is obviously associated with *shemirat miẓvot*. It is no surprise to learn that Adam the Second is far more imbued with religious feeling than Adam the First. He does not pursue functional and operational aims. His desire is not to control his environment, but, rather, to discipline and control himself. His inquiries are of a metaphysical nature: he wants to know the purpose of his own existence as well as that of the surrounding world. Let us cite the author on this point.

> While Adam the First is dynamic and creative, transforming sense data into thought constructs, Adam the Second is receptive and beholds the world in its original dimensions. He looks for the image of God not in the mathematical formula or the natural relational law but in every beam of light, in every bud and bloom, in the morning breeze and the stillness of a starlit evening. In a word, Adam the Second explores not the scientific universe but the irresistibly fascinating qualitative world where he establishes an intimate relation with God.[4]

It follows that dignity and majesty are not the main objectives of Adam the Second. He is characterized by his striving for redemptiveness, or—as the author puts it—"cathartic redemptiveness," which expresses itself in "the feeling of axiological security. The individual intuits his existence as worthwhile, legitimate and adequate, anchored in something stable and unchangeable."[5] It might be added that the adjective "cathartic" refers to the feeling of purification and relief experienced by man when he is certain that he has a meaningful task to fulfill, and his life's purpose is clear to him.

The second Adam is lonely because of his singularity and his deep sense of individuality. On the other hand, he has a feeling of incompleteness and inadequacy, and hence, a craving for association with other human beings. However, the community which he seeks is not the functional-operational one of Adam the First, but what the author calls a "covenantal community" linked together by the *brith*, which constitutes a *kehillah kedoshah* united by religious observance, prayer, and Torah study. To compare once more the two communities formed by Adam the First and Adam the Second:

> Adam the First relates himself to others since communication to him means information about the surface activity of practical man. Such a dialogue certainly cannot quench the burning thirst for communication in depth of Adam the Second, who always will remain a *homo absconditus* (a person concealed) if the majestic logoi of Adam the First should serve as the only medium of expression.[6]

The two Adams are actually interdependent, although the dependence of the first on the second is stressed more. In Rabbi Soloveitchik's view, Adam the First cannot succeed completely in his desire to attain majesty and dignity without the Man of Faith contributing his share. More than that, the author claims that without the cooperation of Adam the Second the civilizational edifice erected by Adam the First would be built on "shifting sands." "Successful Man wants to be a sovereign, not only in the physical, but also in the spiritual world. He is questing not only for material success but also for ideologico-axiological achievement as well."[7] "Since majestic man is in need of a transcendental experience in order to strengthen his cultural edifice, it is the duty of the Man of Faith to provide him with some component parts of this experience."[8] It goes without saying that Adam the First creates the whole complex fabric of civilizational existence, of which Adam the Second is a beneficiary. Human life would be too short, beset with dangers and suffering, were we not to enjoy the achievements of Adam the First.

Then, again, it becomes clear, at the end of Rabbi Soloveitchik's essay, that Adam the First and Adam the Second are no more than typological constructs. In real terms they represent one person, a sort of all-inclusive ideal human personality involved, as it were, in self-confrontation. The pronounced universalist tendency present in Rabbi Soloveitchik's essay has never received the attention it deserves. We have seen that ideal humanity was hermeneutically developed, through the fusion of the two types of Adam. It would, indeed, be an unreasonable assumption were we to submit that, in the author's view, the personality of Adam, or, for that matter, the two types of Adam, are to be conceived of as being exclusively Jewish. The more likely conclusion from the fact that the author's philosophic homily centers around Adam (who is not affiliated with any specific religious denomination) is that real humanity is realizable by man as such, and that this quality of humanity converges with ideal Jewishness.

It goes without saying that the Jewish Man of Faith is nurtured and shaped by Jewish religious sources, which form the mainspring of his spirituality. Men of other faiths depend on their own holy books in the spirit of the prophet Micah: "For all people will walk, everyone in the name of his God, and we will walk in the name of the Lord our God for ever and ever." However, from a structural point of view it is the synthesis of the Man of Faith and the man of practical achievement that is of benefit to man himself as well as to society, and it represents a valid ideal for all.

Soloveitchik's next essay, originally published in Hebrew and entitled "The Man of Halakhah," aims at the characterization of the halakhic personality and, through it, of Judaism as a whole. Written in poetic Hebrew with lyrical overtones, it is composed— as several writers have already observed—in a vein reminiscent of existentialist philosophy. It endeavors to present the most characteristic features of Judaism by describing a personality, unique and complex by nature, capable of ascending to heights of self-realization and excelling in inner freedom, independence, authenticity, and, above all, creativity. These are the main characteristics which Rabbi Soloveitchik attributes, surprisingly, to the Man of Halakhah. If I am asked why "surprisingly," I would reply that the very term Halakhah is associated in our minds with restrictions on human conduct not easily concomitant with freedom, authenticity, and the other qualities which he attributes to the man of Halakhah.

How does Soloveitchik arrive at this conclusion, and what, in particular, is the meaning of the term "creativity," which, conditioned by the presence of the other attributes, constitutes the highest and most important quality of the Man of Halakhah? The importance of creativity is both directly stated and indicated by the exposition which is devoted to this concept as compared with the other attributes. To become truly creative, the Man of Halakhah has first to pass a stage of perception in which he gains knowledge and gathers impressions which help him to embrace the entire scope of his particular discipline. Creativeness is nourished by information gathered from the enormous number and variety of halakhic sources. But more important even than the foregoing is the internalization of the principles in the Kantian sense. The creative stage, following on that of study and cognizant perception, is ushered in by the attempt to apply these principles to real-life situations. This act of application is likened by the rabbi to the application of scientific knowledge in everyday life.

In spite of the similarity of the two processes—the halakhic and the scientific—there are, of course, differences, not only in a methodological but in an essential sense. These are rooted in the divergent character of the two sets of principles: those of Halakhah are transcendental in nature, and are claimed to originate in divine revelation; those of science are conceived by man, they evolve gradually and, thus, are subject to modification in the light of new experience. Halakhic knowledge, with its imprint of the divine will, when applied in our lives, contributes to the absorption of eternity in our temporary existence. In other words, this aspect of creativity in the Man of Halakhah may be metaphorically expressed as causing the Divine Presence to descend and inhabit the physical world and, as a result, elevate worldly life to a higher level of spirituality. As Soloveitchik says: "Creativity—this is the descent of transcendence into our turbid, coarse material world, and this descent is brought about by the incorporation of ideal halakhah in the midst of reality."[9] Further on in his essay he says: "Creativeness is the aim of halakhah and creativity means the realization of eternal halakhah in the temporal and passing world, the 'reduction' (*zimẓum*) of the honor of the Eternal in the midst of human reality, the descent of the Divine presence to the reality pervading our temporary life."[10]

In addition to transposing transcendental principles into the human world, the creativity of the Man of Halakhah is also expressed by the logical manipulation of these principles so that they can be applied to human conditions. In this way, the Man of Halakhah contributes to the perfection of the human world. Soloveitchik bases himself on various rabbinic assertions which claim that God did not create a perfect world, but expected man to contribute to its perfection and thus become His partner in the cosmic process. Any activity which helps to civilize the world, to make it more habitable, more amenable to human requirements, and, on a spiritual plane, any effort to improve the quality of human institutions and relationships—in short, any performance of the duties which man owes to man and to God constitutes a realization of this partnership.

To further elucidate the complex nature of the act of creativity attributed to the Man of Halakhah, he compares him with the religious mystic. The halakhist's creativeness differs from that of the mystic in that it is based on knowledge rather than on religious experience. It is worldly in nature and aimed at the improvement of life on earth. In a metaphorical sense, the direction of the halakhist's activity may be represented as a downward movement, whereas the mystic's aspirations lead, as it were, upwards toward the deity and the world of pure spirit. In the rabbi's words:

Whereas secret wisdom [*kabbalah*] heals the imperfections of the created world by endeavoring to lift it upwards toward the pure and perfect Being, the Halakhah fulfills the same task by causing the *Shekhinah* [Divine Presence] to descend to the human world by the concentration—as it were—of transcendence in the midst of our imperfect world.[11]

In using the kabbalistic phrase "concentration of transcendence," Soloveitchik no doubt wishes to convey the idea that a life permeated by the principles of Halakhah invites, as it were, the Divine Presence to descend and dwell in our midst.

To avoid possible misunderstanding, it should be stated that the term "Man of Halakhah" does not refer exclusively to the rabbinical scholar, but, in a wider sense, also to any Jew who lives by the principles of Halakhah. It is only natural for the acting halakhic scholar to become involved in worldly matters, from examining kashrut arrangements of diverse kinds (even involving blood-stained fingers in examining the lungs of a slaughtered animal) to intervening in marital disputes and dealing with problems arising from the heterogeneous facets of present-day society. He cannot keep aloof from its more unpleasant manifestations but, on the contrary, must be prepared to become involved in them should the need arise. One cannot help being puzzled by the contrast between the worldly nature of the halakhic scholar's activities on one hand, and the spiritual aspects of its effects and implications, i.e., inviting the *Shekhinah* to dwell in our midst, for this, according to Soloveitchik, is precisely the highest goal of the Man of Halakhah.

> The ideal of the man of Halakhah is to cause the Shekhinah to dwell here in our worldly lives—"and there I will meet with thee and speak with thee" [Exodus 25:22]. This verse represents the highest goal of Halakhah.[12]

Apart from becoming involved in human relationships and a host of other everyday matters, the ideal Man of Halakhah is a studious observer of nature in the widest sense. In the essay reviewed here there is a long and poetic description of the marvels of nature perceived by the Man of Halakhah, as well as his reactions and responses to them. What engages his mind are, above all, the seasonal changes and transformations which exercise a profound influence on the life of the observant Jew. Dusk and dawn, sunrise and sunset, weekday and the Sabbath, the new moon, festivals and fasts—all of these reflect the flow of time and the changes occurring in nature. These, in turn, have a bearing on a host of halakhic observances which shape the character of Jewish life.

The highest phase of the halakhist's creativity is attained by him through the process of self-transformation or *teshuvah*, "return" or "penitence," a subject on which the rabbi has held many oral discourses which were later published.[13]

One of the dimensions of creativity attributed to the halakhist is the transformation of chaos into cosmos, as far as the external world is concerned. The process of building up one's personality, in short, self-education, is viewed in a similar way. It is the attempt to transform the inner chaos in man into cosmos in relation to a framework of moral principles. "The highest principle to be adopted by us is the attempt to re-create ourselves. It is Judaism that brought this idea into the world."[14]

The Man of Halakhah is further characterized in the essay under discussion by the independence of mind which colors his religious activities—paradoxical as this may sound in view of the many "thou shalt nots" of Halakhah. According to Soloveitchik, the Man of Halakhah is not dependent on mystical experience or any other kind of supranatural inspiration, but he relies solely on his halakhic scholarship, i.e., the logical manipulation of principles derived from relevant codes and their application to everyday life. This independence is given great prominence, and the Man of Halakhah is lauded precisely because of this attribute.

The man of Halakhah is a ruler in the kingdom of reason and spirit. There is nothing that stands in his way: everything is subject to his arbitration and obeys his judgments. Even the Holy One, blessed be His name, bestows his seal of approval on the halakhist's arbitrations and grants him the imprint of His authority in matters of Torah observance; the Creator of the Universe, as it were, accepts man's halakhic decisions and rulings as valid.[15]

The authority and standing of the Man of Halakhah surpasses that of intellectuals in scientific and other secular fields.

The man of Halakhah wields the highest authority and is admired by every one. . . . no other branch of knowledge has ever crowned its masters in a way comparable to that of Halakhah. In no other intellectual pursuit has the scholar been so highly extolled as the master of Halakhah. The glorification of man here reaches its apotheosis.[16]

These words of praise for the Man of Halakhah, which may sound somewhat exaggerated to the secular-minded, are meant to characterize the ideal *Ish ha-Halakhah* par excellence. It goes without saying that here and there a rabbi falls short of this ideal. Soloveitchik is quite aware of this discrepancy, warning the reader in a footnote at the beginning of the essay:

the characterization of the man of Halakhah refers to the pure ideal type, like other ideal types dealt with in the human sciences. The real men of Halakhah, who are not simple but rather complex types, approximate to the ideal type to a higher or lesser degree as the case may be, dependent on the intellectual and spiritual level of their personalities.[17]

Spontaneity and authenticity are further characteristics of the ideal Man of Halakhah, and both are prerequisites to creativity. Generally speaking, these are the characteristics of persons who hold views and beliefs of their own and are not easily persuaded to give them up in favor of ideas in vogue at any time. Authenticity, in particular, marks the highly developed personality, which is in contrast to "the man of the species" (*ish ha-min*), whose character bears the imprint of generality and tends to uncritical acceptance of the prevailing mores of society.

In sum, the Man of Halakhah is a highly individualized person, independent, authentic, inner-directed, deriving spiritual orientation from the sources of Judaism, which he absorbs and integrates into his being. By contrast, the "man of the species"

does not possess anything that might form the core of his existence as a singular individual and might sustain and legitimize his personality. His roots are anchored in mediocrity . . .

he lacks stature and a profile of his own. He lacks originality and creativity and never brings out anything new. In short, he is receptive and passive, entirely dependent on the ideas and opinions of others.[18]

It is difficult to resist the conclusion that this very distinction that the learned rabbi makes between the Man of Halakhah, on the one hand, and the common man, on the other, reflects the approach of an intellectual aristocrat, which is somewhat surprising in a man of religion, who is expected to regard all his fellow human beings as children of God, equally deserving of tolerance and love. The rabbi's emphasis on creativity, independence, and authenticity, and his distinction between the two categories of man, are reminiscent of certain trends in existentialist philosophy, in particular of the Heideggerian brand. It was Heidegger who differentiated so clearly between the authentic man and the "fallen," undistinguished, commonplace one.[19]

In discussing creativity as the aim of Halakhah, Soloveitchik uses ideas borrowed from Maimonides, yet their formulation is reminiscent of the language of modern philosophers and psychologists. Of his several attempts to sum up the meaning of creativeness I quote the following:

The secret of creativeness rests in the union of receptive and active intelligence. Receptive intelligence is merely passive, serving, as it were, as material upon which the active intelligence imposes a shape. At first, man is receptive, though potentially endowed with active intelligence, and creativity means spontaneity, activeness, originality, innovation, initiative, and daring. Hence, man should become an active and stimulating person. His potential should evolve into actuality, receptiveness into spontaneity. In the creative process, formless and inactive matter is made alive and brought into action. The concept of personal deeds and actions plays an important role in Judaism, and this idea forms the concept of creativeness in the thought of Maimonides.[20]

It is no mere coincidence that the identical qualities—creativity spontaneity, activeness, originality, authenticity—are regarded as values of central importance in secular Western philosophical and educational thought. In spite of the plurality of trends in Western philosophy there seems to be general agreement about the positive character of these values. I do not think that Halakhah and, in a wider sense, Judaism in toto, have ever been characterized in similar terms by other Jewish traditionalist philosophers. This would appear to be a rather novel and original trend in the rabbi's philosophy, its purport being—either deliberately or possibly unconsciously—to convey to the modern Jew that the very same values that underlie secular Western thought are, from a purely structural viewpoint, inherent in fundamental Jewish philosophy and hence not alien to the Jew. "The highest moral and religious perfection which Judaism strives to attain is personified in the creative person."[21] These are striking words and rather surprising when used in the context of a theological essay.

Moreover, religious creativity, as distinct from that of a secular artistic nature, contains a dimension absent from the corresponding secular sphere. The idea of human partnership in divine creation and of endowing worldly life with the attribute of holiness is, of course, entirely specific to religious thought. However, from a purely structural point of view, as distinct from specific content, the ideals of Judaism, far from being opposed to those of Western philosophy, are parallel to it. This creates a link between the two cultures and bears witness to a pronounced universalist tendency, somewhat rare in traditional Jewish philosophy. It may be recalled that Orthodox Jewish thought views Judaism and secular culture as separate and conflicting entities. Though in his weekly *Havdallah* service Rabbi Soloveitchik pronounces with the sincerity of inner conviction the words "who makest the distinction between the holy and the profane, between light and darkness, between Israel and the gentiles," nevertheless, his writings reveal a bold universalist tendency which requires further elucidation and comment.

In a lecture in English entitled "The Synagogue as an Institution and Idea,"[22] Soloveitchik describes, in existential terms, the predicament of man who feels himself to be "a creature of low stature," lonely, insecure, insignificant, nowhere at home, frightened, intimidated. He quotes a passage from the Song of Songs, referring to King Solomon, whom he sees as such a man: "Behold his bed, which is Solomon's, three-score valiant men are round about it, of the valiant of Israel. They all hold swords, being experts in war; every man has his sword upon his thigh because of fear in the night." He interprets the phrase "fear in the night" as characterizing the creaturely existential fear of King Solomon, whom he sees as symbolically representing modern man—enlightened and mighty, rich in achievement, master of the arts and sciences—whose technological skills have made it possible for him to reach out to the stars. Yet modern man, too, is beset by that basic malaise of "fear in the night." Now it is the purpose of prayer to relieve man of this existential dread and bestow upon him a feeling of "at-homeness" and security, in the spirit of "The Lord is with me and I shall not fear."

Prayer is without doubt motivated by existential dread. This is a fundamental tenet common to all existentialist theology, including the Christian, although it may occasion some discomfort to Rabbi Soloveitchik to find himself so close to the theological tenets of other denominations. Here is a passage of striking similarity to Rabbi Soloveitchik's lecture on the synagogue: John Macquarrie deals with Heidegger's philosophy, which, though not religiously orientated, brings us, he holds, to the threshold of religion. On the phenomenon of anxiety Macquarrie has this to say: "For what is this anxiety or dread, this basic malaise, this uneasy restlessness, this feeling of not being at home in the world, this disclosure which shatters the illusory contentment and security of everyday existence, but the *cor inquietum* of Christian experience" which leads man to God.[23]

To come back to Rabbi Soloveitchik: not only does he interpret the idea of the synagogue in a universalist spirit, i.e., as flowing from the existentialist needs of man, but even the idea of exile, hitherto thought of as specifically a part of the fate of the Jewish people, is widened by him and applied to the whole of mankind, who also feel as if they were in exile, homeless, and estranged from their surroundings. From an existentialist point of view, argues the rabbi, the idea of Galut is universal in character, the Jewish exile being merely a reflection of a more general exilic feeling which is part of the human condition. Since man was driven out of Eden this curse of homelessness has rested upon him.

In endeavoring to bring out the universal aspect of Rabbi Soloveitchik's theological thought, I am well aware that he advocates a proud and independent stance for Judaism vis-à-vis Christianity and other monotheistic religions, free from fraternization in a superficially ecumenical spirit. The rabbi's essay "Confrontations" (*Tradition* 6, no. 2 [1964]) will dispel any doubt that may exist on this point. While aware of the danger of oversimplification, I believe that the following quotation from this essay represents a true reflection of his views on the relation of Judaism to Christianity in the practical field of community relations and the cooperation possible within this framework.

The relationship between two communities must be outer-directed and related to the secular orders with which men of faith come face to face. In the secular sphere, we may discuss positions to be taken, ideas to be evolved, and plans to be formulated. In these matters, religious communities may together recommend action to be developed and may seize the initiative to be implemented later by general society. However, our joint engagement in this kind of enterprise must not dull our sense of identity as a faith community. We must always remember that our singular commitment to God and our hope and indomitable will for survival are non-negotiable and non-rationalizable and are not subject to debate and argumentation.

This proud and independent stance of Judaism, as portrayed by Rabbi Soloveitchik, need not divert our attention from the fact that his theological thought, because of its existentialist foundations and undercurrents, reveals clear universalist tendencies. I hope I have shown that they are manifested in his conception of the good life (symbolized by the fusion of the attributes of the two Adams) as well as the educational ideal (stress on creativity, authenticity, inner freedom, etc.). These ideals are, structurally speaking, common to all mankind.

Finally, the concept of prayer as flowing from the condition of man, and the exilic character which is shared, although differently, by Jew and non-Jew, all spell out, I hope convincingly, the universalist undercurrent of his thought. It may be that Rabbi Soloveitchik's proud insistence on the singularity and otherness of Judaism, as manifested in "Confrontations," flows in a dialectical sense from his clear vision of the framework of ideas and beliefs common to all mankind.

This accentuation of the universalist trend in Rabbi Soloveitchik's thought is of significant value in view of the fact that this trend's influence is receding in present-day traditional Judaism and, *a fortiori*, in Israel, where the nationalistic strain is steadily gaining ground.

It goes without saying that a strong universalist impulse is inherent in the very fabric of Hebrew prophecy, and it also finds appropriate expression in rabbinic thought. Many sayings in the various branches of rabbinic literature bear this out, and I should like to quote one example which seems to be particularly relevant and pertinent. I am thinking of the well-known controversy between Rabbi Akiva and Ben-Azzai as to what is to be regarded as the main principle (*klal gadol*) of Judaism. According to Rabbi Akiva it is "Thou shalt love thy neighbor as thyself," which, in rabbinic tradition, refers to *Aḥikha be-miẓvot*, i.e., to your coreligionist. According to Ben-Azzai, however, it is contained in the following verse: "This is the book of the generations of Adam. In the day that God created man, in the likeness of God He made him." According to Ben-Azzai this principle is more universal, more "exalted" (*nisgav*). As the well-known commentator Rabbi Meir Loeb ben Yechiel Michael (the Malbim) says in his commentary: "Because all human beings are linked to one another in one body. All were created in the image of God, so as to present in wholeness and perfection the image of God, who bears, within Himself the souls of all human beings. Thus all mankind form one entity and are like one body composed of various limbs."

It is only natural that this controversy between Rabbi Akiva and Ben-Azzai was continued in different forms by later Jewish philosophers. To quote a few examples: Maimonides represents the universal trend, Yehuda Halevi the national one. Closer to our times it was Moses Mendelssohn and Samson Raphael Hirsch who represent the universal trend, whereas the school of Rabbi Abraham Isaac Hacohen Kook supports the nationalistic one.

We can only be grateful for the literary work of Rabbi Soloveitchik because it contributes to the reinforcement of the universalist trend, thus helping to restore the balance between the two.

8

Tolerance According to the Teaching of Abraham Isaac Hacohen Kook

Judaism does not claim to represent the sole path leading to salvation in this world and the hereafter. Unlike Christianity, it does not countenance missionary activity, regarding the Jewish people as the sole bearers of its specific precepts. According to the teaching of Rabbi Joshua (second generation of tannaim), "the righteous among the gentiles will attain a portion in the world-to-come," as long as they practice the so-called Noachide Laws, which have been regarded as precepts of natural religion.

Clearly, Judaism is the antithesis of polytheism, but it is tolerant of other monotheistic religions and, for that matter, of any philosophy adopted by non-Jews, as long as they aim at fostering human virtues such as justice, mercy, and kindness to others and thus contribute to the civilizing of humanity.

Within Judaism, the Torah is not tolerant of Jews who transgress the Law and violate the Covenant. Needless to say, there are many condemnations of religious transgressions, both in the Bible itself and in rabbinic teaching. Moreover, the rabbis did not refrain from using coercion in order to secure the fulfillment of the Torah. The psychological presupposition to the exercise of coercion is the tacit understanding that all sons and daughters of Israel are actually willing in the depths of their hearts to abide by the Law, and if any of them does not, he or she is deterred from the right path by an evil impulse, which could be controlled by coercion.

It cannot be denied that there is an element of harshness toward the nonobservant Jew in rabbinic teaching that has burdened the relationship between the Orthodox and non-Orthodox to the present day—witness the current scene in Israel with its many regrettable examples of gross intolerance. However, it should be remembered that there are rabbinic utterances tolerant of the nonobservant and even appreciative of their positive qualities.

When speaking of the simple unlearned and even of those who do not observe the precepts of Torah, the rabbis state that often they excel in human virtues, such as loving-kindness in relation to their fellow human beings, and, by reason of this virtue, they will be found worthy of "welcoming the countenance of the *Shekhinah*." In more general terms they state that even those who are seemingly empty of religious content are yet as full of mitzvot as a pomegranate is full of kernels. Again, it is said that one good deed, if performed with a pure heart, may enable a person to acquire a portion in the world-to-come. We read in Deuteronomy that the Almighty shows mercy unto thousands (of generations) of them that love Him and keep His commandments. The rabbis comment upon the Ketiv *mitzvato* (singular), which in their opinion serves as an allusion to the fact that one mitzvah alone, if performed sincerely and consistently, makes the person who fulfills it worthy of divine love and mercy. We also learn that an Israelite, despite his transgressions, yet remains an Israelite, that is to say, does not forfeit the rights and privileges due to him by virtue of his descent. As a general rule the rabbis advise us not to repudiate the sinner completely: "let the left hand repulse, but the right hand always invite back." The rabbis derived this lesson from the regrettable biblical incident involving Elijah and Gehazi as well as Rabbi Yehoshua ben Perakhia and Jesus the Nazarene. When reflecting upon the fate of the latter, the rabbis felt that the religious authority of his time should not have repulsed him completely and should have shown greater willingness to "invite him back." It is possible that had the rabbis been more conciliatory toward him, we might have been spared untold tragic events, hatred, and animosity in future generations, and history might well have taken a different course. No matter whether the story about Jesus as mirrored in the Talmud is historically accurate, the lesson drawn by the rabbis from it is abundantly clear and of great importance.[1]

The present-day distinction between observant and nonobservant Jews corresponds to the distinction in rabbinic times between the sages on one hand and the common people (amme ha-areṣ) on the other. There is ample evidence in talmudic literature of the lack of harmony, even open friction on occasion, between the two. It is to the credit of the rabbis that they relate how on more than one occasion the amme ha-areṣ excelled in the performance of good deeds, in learning, and even in sharpness of wit.

The Midrash Rabbah (Bereshit 32:10) tells the story of how Rabbi Yonathan (first-generation Palestinian amora), when going up to pray in Jerusalem, met a Samaritan who asked him why he was going to pray on "that dunghill" (referring to the surroundings of the Temple, which then lay in ruins) and not on "that blessed mountain" (referring to Mount Gerizim, deemed sacred by the Samaritans). When asked why he considered that mountain blessed, the Samaritan gave as the reason the fact that it had not been inundated by the waters of the flood and was thus set apart from the other mountains.

Rabbi Yonathan was at a loss to disprove the Samaritan's contention, but the man who was leading his ass asked his master for permission to answer. When this permission was granted, the man quoted Genesis 7:19, where it is written, "And all the high mountains were covered." And in case Gerizim is not regarded as a high mountain, the man continued, it was certainly covered by the flood. Rabbi Yonathan immediately dismounted from his ass and made the man ride on it for three miles, applying to him the following three verses: "There shall not be male or female barren among you or among your cattle" (Deuteronomy 7:14). Rabbi Yonathan added "even among your herdsmen." "Thy temples are like a pomegranate split open" (Canticles 6:7). To this Rabbi Yonathan added: "Even the ignorant among you are as full of counterarguments as a pomegranate of kernels," and this is the meaning of the verse "No weapon that is formed against you shall prosper" (Isaiah 54:17).

Professor Ephraim E. Urbach sums up the relationship between the sages and the *amme ha-areṣ* in the following interesting passage:

> The contact of the Sages, in all generations with broad strata of the people of all classes not only led to the discovery of manifestations of estrangement from Judaism, of disrespect for the Torah and precepts, of abuses of the Sages and the like, but also to the revelation of good qualities, of simple faith, of piety and outstanding acts of charity and benevolence on the part of the common people. With the same honesty and candour with which the sources preserved the negative views of the Sages about the *'ammeha-areṣ* and the evidence of the mutual tension between them, they also reported the positive phenomena among the fringe classes of Jewish society, and even cultivated a tradition of stories in which the *'ammeha-areṣ* appear as the teachers of the Sages in virtues, and the reproved become reprovers. These narratives are better evidence of the self-criticism of the Sages in respect of their relationship to other classes than direct statements that speak in praise of the *'ammeha-areṣ*, of their merits, and the duties towards them.[2]

It need not surprise us that the talmudic civilization, which lasted for almost a thousand years, and to which many religious scholars contributed, should display a rich variety of opinion on the subject of relations between observant and nonobservant Jews. In rabbinic times, pluralism of opinions, in legal matters as well as in questions concerning doctrine, was the rule rather than the exception. However, this variety of opinion existed and was tolerated within well-defined and generally accepted limits.

When religious faith was predominant and its truth was accepted by the majority of people, nonobservance of religious precepts was regarded as abhorrent, and the religious code of behavior was backed by sanctions. This fact explains the condemnation of transgressors of the Law and the harsh pronouncements, both in Halakhah and Aggadah, concerning those who throw off the yoke of the commandments. However, a civilization should be judged by its finest, most humane and far-seeing manifestations, which transcend the constraints and limitations of a certain period of time, and of such manifestations there is evidence in rabbinic sources.

I have dealt so far with the individual pronouncements of the rabbis on the relationship of the observant to the nonobservant. The man who in our century developed a religious philosophy of tolerance concerning this relationship was no one other than Chief Rabbi Abraham Isaac Hacohen Kook, but it should be said at the outset that he would have objected to such a neat division between the two. It was Rabbi Kook's belief that the divine light shines upon every individual Jew, and that all the backsliding he witnessed in his time was merely in the nature of error.

> The evil in them [the religiously unobservant] is merely superfi-
> cial, and many of them cleave to the Jewish nation as a whole
> and carry the name of Israel with pride, though they do not
> always know why, but the root of Israel is holy and good,
> prepared to uphold integrity and justice which truly flow from
> divine wisdom.[3]

Like Rabbi Yehuda Halevi, Rabbi Kook believed in a "divine element" inherent in every Jewish soul. Expressed in more rational terms, if such an attempt is at all feasible, one might say that according to Rabbi Kook there is a special religious propensity inherent in every Jew, which, if brought to higher realization, may then develop into emergence of the holy spirit. This being so, the Jew's sinfulness, regrettable and painful as it appeared to Rabbi Kook, is to be viewed only as an aberration, a superficial divergence from the right path, brought about by external circumstances, i.e., the secular spirit of the age absorbed by them, while "the root" remains whole and sound. Rabbi Kook admired the pioneering spirit of the ḥalutzim of the second and third aliyot, whose idealistic philosophy was expressed in arduous physical work, in order to build up the country and make it habitable for increasing numbers of Jews seeking a safe haven in Eretz Israel. He saw their zeal as the transformation of their religious genius into a life of action, in answer to the needs of the time. In spite of their obviously secular way of life, he regarded them as inspired by their religiously oriented past.

It has to be noted that Rabbi Kook regarded the return of the Jewish people to their homeland and the reclamation of the land after centuries of lying waste as the inauguration of a messianic era heralding the coming redemption not only of Israel but of the whole of mankind. In such an era the return of Jews to a religious way of life seemed to him certain, a natural accompaniment of the reawakened national spirit.

Rabbi Kook believed that in such an era there took place what he describes as an "accumulation of holiness," added to by each subsequent generation. Acts of worship, study of the Torah, the selfless deeds of the Zionist pioneers together with those performed by Jews in all walks of life produced a climate of lasting and heightened spirituality. On the other hand, sins, when committed, were ephemeral in nature and turned into nothingness, in the sense that "all the workers of iniquity shall be scattered" (Psalm 92:10). Obviously Rabbi Kook's language when describing these processes is charged with kabbalistic allusions. He quotes *inter alia* the following verse from Zechariah: "O daughters of Jerusalem, behold thy king cometh unto thee; he is just and having salvation; lonely and riding upon an ass and upon a colt, the foal of an ass."[4]

In the reference to the king riding upon an ass, ritually an unclean animal, Kook sees an analogy to the coming of the Messiah on the backs of the religiously estranged *halutzim* and not on those of the pious Jews. Here there is implied the suggestion that the pious failed to support the reclamation of the Holy Land, just as, at the time of the second commonwealth, it was the simple and unlearned people, according to Kook, who followed Erza and Nehemiah's leadership in the return from Babylon, while the pious (the Levites) preferred exile.

In spite of Kook's admiration for the reclaimers of the land of Israel, he was deeply grieved by their irreligious conduct, inveighing against such breaches as their desecration of the Sabbath and their nonobservance of the dietary laws. For him the observance of religious law was the essential element of the Jewish national consciousness and the main authentic manifestation of the soul of Judaism, for which there could be no substitute. His viewpoint was diametrically opposed to that of Zionists like the poet Avraham Shlonsky, who considered the work of the pioneers as the modern equivalent of the traditional fulfillment of religious commandments. Shlonsky, for example, saw the building of roads in Eretz Israel as superseding prayer and the donning of phylacteries.

In spite of Rabbi Kook's highly comprehensive vision of Judaism (he mastered not only the complete halakhic civilization but also *Mussar, Hasidut,* philosophy, and above all Kabbalah), he regarded, the world of Halakhah as Judaism's very core and sine qua non. His stance on this issue is eloquently brought out in the following passage:

> The contempt for religious precepts . . . has reached a climax in our generation. It has affected the majority of our young people, who do not yet properly know the reason for this rebelliousness; but to the observant eye examining this phenomenon closely, the young are found to be suffering from an old malaise which in former times struck individuals, either few or many. It is a malaise characterized by contempt for observance of the law, which eventually results in Jewish self-hatred. The spiritual independence of the Jewish people, their continued existence, their psychological content, their hope and political standing, all these rest on the basis of the divine law in its beauty and perfection and the sanctity of its precepts. The instinctive recognition of the Jewish people is so deep and so clear that (if need be) they are prepared to choose martydom gladly, knowing that their unique character, their ultimate victory and glory depend on, and are linked with, the holiness of their love for the divine law. [5]

Rabbi Kook extended the hand of friendship to all who entered into dialogue with him, including his ideological adversaries, for whose Zionist idealism he nurtured a warm admiration. He was deeply concerned to bring them back to the recognition of traditional values. And even though he did not succeed in this, he did gain the respect of the secularists. He considered the separation of the Orthodox from the rest of the new Yishuv as totally unwarranted and a grave sin.

It cannot be denied that Rabbi Kook's philosophy of tolerance is steeped in mysticism. Moreover, his philosophy mirrors a particular historical situation that no longer obtains. But it seems to me that these facts do not cancel the validity of his basic principle of the need for tolerance and harmonious co-existence, although it is possible that were he alive today, he would support his belief in tolerance with an additional set of arguments.

Peaceful co-existence of the religious and secular sections of the Israeli population, based on mutual respect and willingness to cooperate, involving compromise on both sides, is the *unum necesarium* of present-day life in an existential sense. Any philosophical conception capable of supporting and maintaining such co-existence should be welcomed.

9

Equality of Women

Much has been written about the role of women in Judaism, and the literature on this subject may be classified according to the writers' dominant objectives. Not surprisingly, many complaints are heard about the various inequalities of women alleged to follow from Hebraic law, particularly with regard to personal status in matters of marriage and divorce, disabilities in communal affairs, such as the right to be elected to representative bodies of religious institutions, and discrimination with regard to status in the field of Jewish learning. Orthodox writers are inclined to minimize or explain away these disabilities while at the same time yielding to criticisms in their endeavors to ameliorate the situation by means of various halakhic devices. A small group of Orthodox philosophers and jurists would do away with these inequalities altogether, while supporting their arguments by halakhic considerations. One of the most articulate and vociferous of these is Yeshayahu Leibowitz.

In his view, the fact that men and women do not have identical religious obligations does not in itself constitute discrimination. Halakhically speaking, women are exempt from those positive commandments which are dependent on time, i.e., whose fulfillment is restricted to certain times of the day or to certain seasons, such as the wearing of ritual fringes and phylacteries or dwelling in a succah. The differentiation of religious obligation

117

according to sex or tribal descent (Cohen, Levi, Israelite) does not per se represent religious discrimination. An Israelite need not view himself as religiously inferior because he is not ritually defiled through contact with a dead body, or for that matter, by being permitted to marry a divorcee. Leibowitz claims that these and similar prohibitions do not possess rationally feasible intrinsic value and derive their religious validity solely from being divinely ordained. It follows that if by divine ordinance there is to be a distinction in such religious obligations according to tribal descent or sex, this in itself need not be regarded as discrimination.

The main reason for the discrimination against women is, according to Leibowitz, rooted in their being exempted from the duty of studying the Torah. Not to be knowledgeable in things Jewish, not to be versed in matters of Jewish religious law and culture, creates a serious handicap which perpetuates a state of inferiority vis-à-vis the male. It goes without saying that such a state of affairs is incompatible with the spirit of our time.

Leibowitz points out that the biased acceptance of female inferiority existed in most cultures up to the very dawn of modern times.

It was universally believed that the culture of the spirit is a male concern and not a generally human one. Even the accepted Halakhah which assigns to woman a high status as a human being—much higher than that allotted to her in the classical Greek world—viewing with very high appreciation her functions in the existential framework of human life within the home and family, this same Halakhah does not allot to her the status of partnership with man in upholding spiritual life.[1]

This inequality lies at the root of all the other anomalies in both the religious and civil status of women. The belief in female inferiority has been adopted from foreign cultures and does not flow from indigenous conceptions in Judaic lore. To maintain and perpetuate such disabilities undermines and disrupts Orthodox Jewish society. Leibowitz is obviously aware of the fact that his demands for the abrogation of these inequalities in one blow, as it were, would, if accepted, revolutionize the whole fabric of Orthodox Jewish life and do away with some of its obsolete manifestations.

It may be pointed out that much has already occurred in the last decades in order to advance the equality of women, and, needless to say, the present state of Jewish education is a far cry from the mishnaic pronouncement that "to teach woman Torah is tantamount to teaching her lewdness" (Sotah 3:4). Leibowitz admits that the present-day *ulpanot* for girls, as well as other Jewish-study institutions for women which have sprung up in Israel and the United States, represent an important step in the right direction, although they do not satisfy his demands. His ideal are Jewish institutions of higher learning in which men and women study side by side—coeducational yeshivot, as it were—an extreme innovation, particularly if viewed against the background of the history of Jewish education in Israel.

In view of Leibowitz's severe strictures on women's education in Orthodox circles, it is necessary to briefly review the present position of woman within the educational system. Even the ultra-Orthodox girls' schools of Agudat Israel are staffed by women teachers who are trained to a fairly high standard in Jewish studies which enables them to fulfill their educational tasks intelligently and effectively. The state religious schools, as well as those belonging to the general trend, are also staffed by women teachers who, *inter alia*, teach Judaic subjects, including Aggadah, Mishnah, and in some cases even Talmud. Moreover, a number of women professors in the faculties of Israeli universities teach Bible, Jewish history, Jewish philosophy, and Kabbalah. These facts alone illustrate the profound change that has occurred in Jewish education of all trends, including the Orthodox. However, in fairness, Leibowitz is undoubtedly aware of these facts. What he objects to is the halakhic exemption of women from Talmud Torah, which has lasted for many centuries and which corresponds to other religious disabilities within Hebraic law. Not all of these are connected with this halakhic exemption, and one cannot resist the impression that Leibowitz places too much emphasis on this point. But inequalities exist, and Leibowitz is justified in highlighting the problem they present. He claims that the whole question should be considered in the light of our own needs and aspirations, and not according to the ruling of ancient codes. In our time all political, social, and intellectual issues apply equally to men and women, and it would be unjust and even fraught with danger if we were to perpetuate a state of affairs which arose from entirely different historical and social conditions. "We, who are determined to uphold the Torah, cannot accept a conception rooted in halakhic decisions which are related to a social reality by no means similar to our own."[2]

Leibowitz has been criticized for advocating halakhic innovations whose rationale is based on historical considerations. It is alleged that by doing so he is on dangerous ground, for similar historical arguments may be applied to many other aspects of Jewish law. Many a mitzvah may be explained, even explained away, by reference to analogous phenomena advanced by the historian, anthropologist, and student of comparative religion. The dietary laws, the laws relating to marital life, and even those relating to the status of non-Jews in Hebraic law—they and many other issues may be undermined by applying to them the method of historical investigation. There can be no doubt that Leibowitz himself would strongly object to such wide-ranging endeavors at reform.

In contrast to Leibowitz's sweeping advocacy—which retains a measure of justification in spite of the criticism just mentioned—the methodological approach to the same problem of a number of Orthodox Jewish legalists (men such as Menachem Elon, Eliezer Berkovits, and Ze'ev Falk) is more cautious and in line with traditional halakhic argument, such as we find employed, for instance, in the responsa literature.

It would be impossible, even unwarranted, in this context, to review the whole body of recent halakhic literature on the place of women in Hebraic law with special reference to the problems arising from their basic inequalities. Suffice to observe that the aforementioned legal scholars generally argue their case on the strength of precedent, analogy, and parallel ruling mentioned in talmudic and post-talmudic literature, and they usually point to change of accepted halakhic ruling by way of *takanot* (enactments), *gezeirot* (precautionary edicts), and *hora'at sha'ah* (emergency laws). They argue, quite rightly, that change of law within carefully guarded limits is inherent in Hebrew law and has always been practiced. Indeed these new enactments have become an important integral part of Hebrew law concerning a host of legal issues. By such means newly arising problems and exigencies have become amenable to solution in the process of time.

The number of such enactments mentioned in the Talmud and post-talmudic legal literature is legion, and a few examples may suffice.

The first mishnah in Tractate *Gittin* states that if a bill of divorce (*get*) is brought to the land of Israel from abroad, then the bearer is required to declare, "In my presence it was written, and in my presence it was signed"; the reason being that a *get* has to be written *li-sh'mo*, i.e., for the particular woman for whom it is intended. If written in Israel, it may be taken for granted that the rabbinical court is acquainted with this requirement—the rule of special intention—but the law courts abroad may not be sufficiently versed in halakhic matters to be conversant with this requirement. Hence the stipulation that the bearer declare that the *get* was written and signed in his presence. Yet the Talmud recounts that in the course of time when such a *get* was brought to Eretz Israel from abroad, Rabbi Yehoshua ben Levi (first-generation Palestinian amora) ruled that the bearer was no longer required to declare that he was present when the *get* was signed. Obviously this was a legal relaxation, motivated by the fact that the rule of special intention had become universally known, unlike previous times, when such an assumption would not necessarily have been justified.

This *takanah*, known to every talmudic student, is quoted by Ze'ev Falk in a chapter dealing with the influence of the changing times on Halakhah,[3] and it is interesting for two reasons: one, it perfectly suits the subject of his chapter, namely, the changing of halakhic rule in the wake of changing circumstances. The second point of interest is specially brought out by the author, who draws attention to the fact that in the case under discussion later generations were appraised as being better versed in legal matters than previous ones, contrary to the generally accepted rabbinic assumption of a steady erosion and decline in man's spiritual stature with the passing of generations.

My second example refers to a rabbinic enactment passed in the

Middle Ages, during the time of Rabbi Meir Rothenburg (1220–1293), and mentioned by the late Isidor Epstein, former principal of Jews' College, London.[4]

According to talmudic law no claim for money can be enforced against married women, since they have no sole property rights, and husbands cannot be held answerable for separate and independent financial transactions of wives. However, with changed conditions this law could not be allowed to remain in force without paralyzing trading operations. The rabbis, realizing the gravity of the problem, ruled that women were to be regarded as agents acting on behalf of their husbands, who were, accordingly, deemed responsible for any liability incurred by their wives.

The last example does not concern the role of women in Jewish law, but it may serve to illuminate the problem. It deals with the talmudic ruling, either based on or linked with the interpretation of the following scriptural verse: "And the Lord said unto Moses: Write thou these words, for after the tenor of these words I have made a covenant with thee and with Israel" (Exodus 34:27). This verse is interpreted by the rabbis as implying that matters transmitted orally ("after the tenor of these words") may not be committed to writing. In other words, they were to be transmitted solely by word of mouth from teacher to pupil, from father to son. But the passage of time and changing circumstances impeded, even inhibited, the observance of this prohibition, as in times of war, when parents and children were separated, or for some other reason; hence an emergency law (*hora'at sha'ah*) was promulgated, based on the scriptural pronouncement, "It is time to work for the Lord, for they have made void Thy law" (Psalm 119:126). Thus the prohibition was in fact abolished, and the whole corpus of the oral law was committed to writing, and parts of it could also be recorded for the purpose of study or instruction.

To return to Leibowitz: The exclusion of women from the study of Torah is similar to the previously quoted prohibition, also based on or linked to a scriptural verse, "And thou shalt teach them diligently unto thy sons" (Deuteronomy 6:7), which is interpreted as meaning sons and not daughters. As already stated, Leibowitz has a point to argue when claiming that the disabilities of women in Jewish law are linked with their preclusion from the study of Torah. This state of affairs, if applied to modern times, represents a serious danger to Orthodox Jewish society. Hence the application of a *hora'at sha'ah* enactment which establishes the equal status of women and men within reasonable limits (Orthodoxy will, for example, not accept acting female rabbis) is justified. This enactment, however, is unlikely to be adopted in one leap, as Leibowitz suggests, in view of the extreme caution of the rabbis and their reluctance to introduce halakhic innovations. It is more likely that amelioration of the disabilities will occur as a gradual process which will be sanctioned by the tacit consent of the rabbinate—more in the nature of a *de facto* than *de jure* legislation. I am reminded of a talmudic pronouncement which places trust not only in people's memories of halakhic detail, as the Talmud shows, but—more importantly still—in their good sense. The rabbis say, "But leave it to Israel; if they are not prophets, yet they are the children of prophets" (*Pesachim* 66a). This I should like to combine with a quotation from Rabbi Yannai, Palestinian amora of the first generation: "If the Torah had been given in an incisively defined [*hatukhah*] manner, the world would have no foot to stand on" (Jerushalmi, *Sanhedrin* 4:2). In other words, if the Torah were to be viewed as a rigidly fixed text, not susceptible to various interpretations, it would in the course of time become irrelevant to our lives. This in turn would undermine the foundations of our existence.

10

Democracy and Religious Freedom

In talks with the late President of Czechoslovakia, Thomas G. Masaryk, the Czech writer Karel Čapek reports that Masaryk regarded the biblical doctrine of man having been created in the image of God, his spirituality and dignity, as lying at the heart of democracy. Of all forms of government, only democracy could uphold these beliefs and affirm the ideals of human equality and dignity; thus democracy, in secular terms, is the corollary of the biblical idea of man's God-likeness and immortality. In his words, "An immortal being cannot be indifferent to another one, and must not exploit, nor oppress him."[1]

Obviously, had Masaryk intended to give a full account of the origin of democracy, he would certainly not have omitted a reference to the fact that the term "democracy," literally "rule of the people," refers to the self-government originally practiced in ancient Athens. It can be assumed that what he intended to emphasize was the decisive Hebraic contribution to the concept of democracy, which is not universally acknowledged by political philosophers.

Though ancient Israel was a monarchy for a long period of time, it might be termed a constitutional monarchy, because in theory and often also in practice, it absorbed, in a manner characteristic of its age, some of the constitutive elements of democracy. Thus, the king was subject to the law like any other citizen, and though he enjoyed privileges, he was warned "that his heart be not lifted

124

up above his brethren and that he turn not aside from the commandments to the right hand nor to the left" (Deuteronomy 17:20). There is no need to recount the numerous instances when Hebrew kings were severely reprimanded by the prophets of Israel for the iniquities which resulted from their disregard of the law by which they were solemnly enjoined to abide. One might say that the *whole* Book of Kings is one long reprimand. Unlike the despots of ancient times as well as later ages, the Hebrew king was commanded "to write out a copy of the law and read therein all the days of his life," as a reminder of his subjection to a higher authority. These restrictions on absolute power are detailed in the Talmud, among them the injunction to consult with the Sanhedrin on major policy decisions, such as almost every declaration of war.

The very idea of the Covenant between God and the forefathers of the Hebrew nation, and later the Sinaitic Covenant between God and the whole people of Israel, was an acceptance, free of coercion, similar to the adoption of a constitution of binding character by a modern-day people. Moreover, the delegation of power mentioned in Exodus, and accepted by Moses at the initial molding of the people into a nation, represents a democratic conception developed in later ages. Another democratic feature of ancient Hebrew history was the decisive character of majority rule (Deuteronomy 23:1), which prevailed whenever there was a conflict of opinions between judges in both religious and civil matters, a principle which in later times has lent itself to considerable extension in all matters of public concern.

One of the leaders of American Jewry at the beginning of this century, Judge Mayer Sulzberger, goes so far as to claim that representative government owes its origin mainly to the genius of the Hebrew people.

The Jewish people at large had as keen an outlook and as wide a vision in political as in religious affairs; and while the modern monotheistic conception of the universe is largely the product of their genius, so the modern conception of a rational democratic representative government owes its origin to the same ancestry.[2]

Judge Sulzberger concludes his essay with the following comment:

> There is no historical record of any other nation which as early as a millennium before the present era had overcome the forces of both despotism and of unbridled democracy. Israel alone had with prophetic instinct anticipated the political and religious development which was to come into its own after thousands of years.[3]

There is no doubt that the findings of Judge Sulzberger, not unlike those of Masaryk, tend to extol the Hebraic contribution and thereby consciously or unconsciously diminish the contribution of Greek political philosophy. But the Hebraic contribution to the conception of democracy cannot be denied, and it is possible to claim that the founders of the modern State of Israel, when adopting a democratic system, did so not only because they were influenced by Central and Western European democracies, but because the concept of democracy is deeply rooted in the Hebraic heritage. It could also be argued that the demographic changes which have in many ways affected the State of Israel during recent decades will not deflect the leaders of the state from a fundamentally democratic orientation.[4]

To accept that democracy is the most congenial form of government to the Jewish people does not necessarily imply a neat separation between state and religion as found in the United States. What this concept does imply is, to use Lincoln's formula, government of the people, by the people, for the people. With regard to the safeguarding of citizens' liberties one might say—leaning on John Stuart Mill's famous essay "On Liberty"—that the concept of democracy implies freedom of conscience in the broadest sense, including the expression and publication of opinions on any subject; liberty to plan and shape one's life to suit one's desires and aspirations; and finally the right to unite with other people in forming political parties, alignments, or coalitions in pursuance of political, social, and religious aims. These—along with the separation of the three branches of government: executive, legislative, and judicial—are the essentials of true democracy, which have been somewhat whittled away by the welfare state even in the most advanced democratic countries.[5] In any case it may be argued that the concept of democracy allows for variation of procedures in matters of public concern, including arrangements regarding education and the place of religion in the state.

The attempt to include in the legal structure of Israel, elements borrowed from the Jewish heritage which has shaped the nation's civilization for many centuries, does not in itself represent an infringement of the spirit of democracy. And there has been no objection to the adoption of religious symbols, such as the biblical Menorah as the symbol of the State of Israel, or the Star of David for Israel's flag. Even in matters of religious legislation, a far more serious issue than ceremonial symbols, there are laws adopted by the Knesset and enforced by the state which are supported by a consensus of the Israeli population. The institution of Shabbat as the official day of rest in the Shabbat public-observance laws, insistence on the supply of kosher food to all government and municipal institutions, including the army as well as in Israeli airlines, and government support for religious schools, including those of the independent Orthodox trend, are all examples of the general acceptance of religious principles by the people of Israel. In countries such as America, there is no government support for religious education, for the state neither finances religious activities nor does it intervene in religious education—the two criteria that are the hallmark of the separation of state and religion.

In discussing government support for religious institutions in Israel, mention should be made of the "religious councils" responsible for such activities as divine service, the appointment of rabbis, religious courts, their judges and clerical staff. These councils are semiautonomous institutions supported by local authorities and government departments—the Ministries of the Interior and Religion. The members of these councils are generally observant Jews belonging to religious political parties; some are, however, recruited from secular parties in order to represent the interests of the general population in matters of religion. The latter parties claim that religious institutions should not be merely the concern of religious parties, since the wider Israeli population also makes use of the services provided and contributes to their upkeep. Here again there is acceptance of the fact that the religious councils should be maintained by public funds. As a matter of fact, the majority of the Israeli population, which does not identify with the religious parties, wants more representation on these bodies and firmer control of their activities and finances.

So much for the practically noncontroversial involvement of religion in Israeli public life. As far as the individual citizen is concerned, there is, needless to say, no interference whatsoever in his personal convictions. The outside observer may not always be aware that the individual citizen, notwithstanding the influence of religious laws on government and municipal bodies, has complete freedom in such matters.

As the late Jacob Herzog points out:

> Even the most extreme faction in the religious bloc has declared more than once that its religious demands relate solely to government and municipalities and by no means to the citizen's personal life. They have asked that public policy in the state should give expression to Jewish tradition so that the country as such would preserve a distinctive Israeli character. They see in this an affirmation of our historic continuity, an emphasis on the distinctiveness of our nationhood, and a tribute to our heritage, without which, they believe, the nation is liable to lose its native bearings and the link between Israel and the Diaspora would be weakened beyond any tangible identification.[6]

On the other hand, it would be incorrect to claim that the Law of Marriage and Divorce enacted and enforced in Israel does not impinge upon the beliefs and convictions of the individual. Objections have been raised by the nonreligious people to the very fact that the state imposes a religious ceremony on people who may not believe in it, and to whom at any rate it appears devoid of meaning. Moreover, opposition is greatest not to the religious marriage ceremony as such, but to the fact that it is the only form of marriage performed in Israel which is recognized and registered by the state. It has to be recalled that the only marriage ceremonies recognized are those performed by an Orthodox rabbi, whereas rabbis belonging to other streams in Judaism are excluded.

Professor Nathan Rotenstreich objects to the imposition by the state of a religious marriage ceremony.

> Measured by the standard of sincerity, a marriage contract sanctioned by an authority which the couple does not recognize, cannot be acknowledged without compromising one's principles and without practicing some measure of duplicity. How can a marriage contract be represented as authentic when the couple is forced to choose either the frying pan of no social sanction of their bond or the fire of religious sanction.[7]

It is possible that Rotenstreich, under present circumstances, would feel less strongly on this issue. Today the number of couples who do without formal sanction of their union is legion, not because of opposition to a religious ceremony but for various practical reasons, including a preference for noncommitment.

That the acceptance of a Jewish religious marriage ceremony may be viewed in an entirely different light from that presented by Nathan Rotenstreich can be gathered from the following passage in Herzog's book:

> For non-believing Jews the Jewish marriage and divorce ceremonies involve no denial whatsoever of their non-religious convictions. The participants in these ceremonies are not required to make any declaration of religious faith. Nor is such belief considered necessary for the validity of the act in question. The non-believing Jew may choose to see in these ceremonies a national form rather than a religious prescription and in subscribing to this form he has the satisfaction of knowing that he is sustaining the essential spiritual unity of the nation.[8]

As already mentioned, the Law of Marriage and Divorce has been criticized, even opposed, not only because it establishes the religious ceremony as the only one recognized by the state, but because it equates religious marriage with the Orthodox interpretation, thus discriminating against other trends in Judaism, such as the Conservative and Reform. It is held that because of their permissive attitude in matters of religious law, if the progressive streams in Judaism were granted the right to perform marriage and divorce ceremonies, this would be tantamount to the state condoning civil marriage and divorce. Thus the issue of civil marriage and that of religious pluralism in the fullest sense of the term are closely linked.

In other respects there is complete religious freedom in Israel, and Conservative and Reform congregations do exist and enjoy full autonomy, worshipping and teaching in accordance with the principles of their faith. Their rabbis, however, are not given the right to perform marriage and divorce ceremonies, or to act as religious judges. This right has so far been withheld because of the widespread feelings among Orthodox Jews in Israel and the Diaspora (Israeli Orthodoxy being represented in the Knesset and government by the religious parties) that the state cannot afford a liberal, permissive attitude in matters of marriage and divorce because of the precarious situation of the Jewish people, especially in the Diaspora, where the community's existence is threatened not only by an extremely low birthrate, but also by the frequency of mixed marriages and the rapid assimilation to which they lead.

Nathan Rotenstreich argues that marriage out of the faith merely marks the culmination of an already existing process of assimilation, which cannot be halted by a religious veto. There is some truth in this contention; however, it cannot be denied that leniency on the part of the religious authorities in Israel on this sensitive issue would contribute to the legitimization of mixed marriages and thus serve to encourage them. It must be borne in mind that Diaspora Jewry views the State of Israel as one of the main pillars safeguarding the continued existence of the Jewish people.[9] The leaders of Israel, for their part, feel a special responsibility for the spiritual and physical well-being of Diaspora Jewry, and therefore refrain from setting an example which would adversely affect the religious identity of Diaspora Jewry.

In the days of Ben-Gurion the question of "Who is a Jew?"—an issue of fundamental importance which reaches down to the

existential roots of the Jewish people—aroused fierce and pro-
tracted controversy. The relevance of this to the Law of Return is
obvious, but it also has an immediate bearing on matters of
marriage, personal status, and a number of other issues, such as
military service, etc. The seriousness of this issue caused Ben-
Gurion to turn for advice to the "Sages of Israel"—renowned
scholars of Judaism in Israel as well as the Diaspora. The overwhelming majority confirmed the halakhic viewpoint, declaring
that a Jew is a person born of a Jewish mother or a person who
was converted to Judaism by recognized rabbinical authorities.
At that time the question arose as a sequel to the by now *cause
célèbre* of Brother Daniel Rufeisen, a Dominican monk of Jewish
descent, who claimed that, being a Jew by birth, the Law of
Return applied to him as it does to any other Hebrew, and Israeli
citizenship should have been granted to him automatically, not
by naturalization. The decision of the High Court of Justice went
against the halakhic ruling, and the "Jewishness" of Brother
Daniel was not recognized. The High Court ruled most sophisti-
cately that, since the Law of Return was promulgated by a secular
body, the legal decision was guided by the commonsense point of
view which refuses to regard a Christian monk as a Jew even if he
happens to be of Jewish parentage, and not by the halakhic
conception.[10]

The Shabbat public-observance laws instituted by the Knesset,
which prohibit public transportation on the Shabbat, cause in-
convenience to some Israelis. It is ironic that the most vociferous
opponents of this law are well-to-do Israelis who own private cars
and do not depend on public transportation during the week.
However, there is no violation of religious conscience as a result of
this law, although it may possibly cause a measure of inconve-
nience to some citizens. This applies also to the closing of cin-
emas, theaters, cafes, etc., on the Shabbat. Nevertheless, both
the marriage and divorce laws and the Shabbat observance laws
have become part of the status quo sanctioned by custom. They
are either accepted or acquiesced to, sometimes rather grudg-
ingly, and rarely arouse public controversy. There is, however, a
strong demand for a lenient interpretation of both laws by the
religious authorities.

Mention should also be made of the Law of Anatomy and

Pathology, which has aroused controversy because it allows for an exemption from postmortem examination on religious grounds—if the deceased, when alive, expressed the wish not to have it performed, or failing that, if his family objects. This law can hardly be characterized as antidemocratic, because it provides for maximal consideration of individual wishes in this matter. Criticism of this law was based on medical opinion which regards it as incompatible with the demands of modern medical research.

More severe opposition has been voiced against the law which limits abortions to cases where there is serious danger to the life of the mother, while precluding it on social or economic grounds. This limitation has been opposed not only in feminist circles, but by all those who hold that a woman should be the sole arbiter in matters concerning her own body and it is not for the state to interfere.

Finally, the prohibition against archaeological excavations if and when the remains of ancient graveyards are actually found, or their existence is surmised, has also aroused sharp controversy, involving the media, both in the Knesset and in academic circles.

Inevitably there are problems arising from alleged contravention of the religious ordinances sanctioned by the state. They tend to make the headlines and capture the attention of the public at large. There are also problems of a different kind: a couple registers for marriage at the rabbinate and learns that their union is prevented through insurmountable halakhic difficulties, as when a Cohen wishes to marry a divorcee, when the conversion to Judaism of one of the partners is questionable, or if any other act is brought to light which, halakhically speaking, precludes the performance of a marriage ceremony. Finally, halakhic injunctions even impinge upon matters of burial, as attested in a recent controversy over the interment of a non-Jewish person in a Jewish cemetery.

It is hardly surprising that whenever such problems arise, the question of the involvement of religion in state legislation is reopened and passionately debated in the Knesset, the press, and the other media. A source of exacerbation is that at least some of the religious laws have been adopted under conditions which resemble negotiations under duress. Since no political party in Israel has so far attained an absolute majority, the relatively larger one is compelled to form a coalition with smaller parties, notably the religious ones, which hold the balance. These parties are then in a position to demand, as *conditio sine qua non* for joining a coalition, religious concessions which the majority party, if acting alone, might not otherwise have conceded. For some the very concept of a coalition government activates forces and gives rise to a situation which they see as an infringement of democracy.

This description attempts to set out the present situation, without overrating or minimizing the dimensions of the problem. The impartial observer in Israel might well ask himself whether a disengagement between religion and state does not offer a better solution to the problem, by safeguarding greater freedom in matters of religion and thus completely eliminating religious coercion. My answer is in the negative, though I admit that a separation of state and religion would radically eliminate religious coercion. Nevertheless, I shall try to present the case against separation as objectively as I can and support it by a set of arguments whose rationale is not confined to believers in religious Orthodoxy, but may claim adherents among a wider range of opinion.

1. Judaism is an all-embracing religion, relevant not only to the individual but to the community as a whole. Hence it may rightly be expected that in a state calling itself Jewish the spirit of Judaism should imprint itself on public life by way of religiously orientated legislative action. The maxim of "rendering unto God that which belongs to Him and unto Caesar what belongs to Caesar" is based on a sharp division of spheres, spiritual and worldly, alien to the spirit of Judaism. Moreover, the idea of the Covenant between God and Israel, so central to Jewish doctrine, emphasizes the fact that the individual's identification with the people as a whole is part and parcel of his own individual Jewish consciousness. Monastic asceticism and the solitude of a private existence are not Jewish ideals; either "fellowship or death" is, according to the Talmud (*Ta'anit* 23a), the motto of Judaism.

2. A separation of state and religion would further deepen the rift between the religious and secular elements of Israel's popula-

tion even to the point where marriage between members of the two sectors would become halakhically problematical. Since civil divorce has no religious validity, it may leave a divorcee in her previous marital state and hence would render illegitimate the offspring of a remarriage. This is only one of the many problems that would arise if there were a division between state and religion. A more pessimistic forecast would be the eventual emergence of two separate Jewish nations. It is obvious that such a development would be fraught with danger, the avoidance of which calls for a readiness to compromise on both sides: the secular sector of the community might be expected to forgo its demand for absolute freedom from religious legislation, while the religious community would have to renounce its excessive demands for the promulgation of religious laws.

3. The disestablishment of state religion would lead to an intensified process of secularization, which, in turn, would bring about a breach of historical continuity and the loss of Israel's specifically Jewish character, to the point of endangering the survival of the Jews. The connection with the Diaspora, where Judaism and Jewish identity express themselves mostly in religious terms, however tenuous, is vital for the Jews' survival as a people. An entirely secularized Israel, whose identity is nationally orientated, using the Hebrew language and with a secular Hebrew culture, would become alienated from fellow-Jews in the Diaspora.

4. Though the Orthodox are famed for stubbornly clinging to their Jewish heritage, even under adverse conditions, they too would emerge as losers in the event of a separation of state and religion, not only on economic grounds, but also for painful ideological reasons in view of the potential rift within the Jewish people. Economically, their religious institutions, kindergartens, schools, yeshivot, and kolelim would no longer be lavishly supported by the government, and it would be extremely difficult to maintain these institutions on voluntary donations alone.

5. Apart from the economic threat to religious institutions in the event of the disestablishment of religion, there is a widely felt anxiety in religious circles that once the separation of state and religion has taken place, there is no telling how far the process of

secularization will go. The Knesset may institute laws which represent a serious challenge to traditional religious values and slowly deprive the Jewish state of its *differentia specifica*. Thus Israel might turn into an inglorious copy of other European ministates like Luxembourg or Monaco or Lebanon! Already in the past the most vociferous controversies were engendered by the Knesset's attempts to introduce laws which offended values hallowed by Jewish tradition.

6. Finally, there is no evidence that the majority of Israeli citizens are in favor of separation of the state from religion. The evidence so far seems to point in the opposite direction, provided of course that there is no substantial deviation from the status quo as established by Ben-Gurion and generally acquiesced to. At present the majority of Israel's population is of oriental origin and considers such a separation contrary to its deeply ingrained feelings about Jewishness. Even in the Ashkenazi community, there are, apart from the Orthodox, a considerable number of traditional Jews (*mesorati'im*) who wish to retain the specifically Jewish character of the state. Then there are nonobservant Jews who, in view of their nationally orientated *Weltanschauung*, approve of the state's support of Judaism in its widest sense. This they consider not only desirable but a natural matter of course.

There is, however, a determined minority of articulate and vociferous secularists who regard the abolition of the present religious establishment as a major item on their ideological agenda. They claim that the Zionist movement understood itself as being the antithesis of religious Judaism, and envisaged as the ultimate goal of Zionism the creation of a secular state uninfluenced by religious law and custom in its day-to-day life. Historically speaking this is only partly true, for the Zionist ideology was, in a religious sense, never of one piece, but was made up of secular as well as religiously orientated elements. It must be conceded, though, that the latter joined the Zionist movement rather late. Moreover, the question of the religious roots of the yearning for Zion and their influence on the Zionist movement (in spite of the opposition of Orthodox leaders) has been fully explicated and resolved and has to be regarded as an established fact.

In addition, some of the secularists claim that there can be no compromise on matters of individual freedom—this must be respected even if there is a majority in favor of its limitation in such matters as personal status, etc. They cannot be persuaded to accept the present state of affairs on the basis of an analysis of the characteristics of Judaism because of their *a priori* rejection of a religiously tinged conception of Israeli statehood. Some of them deny the inseparability of nationhood and religion in Judaism. For example, several of their leaders have protested vigorously against the requirement to state that they are Jews by religion in the recently distributed census form, for according to their convictions they are Jews by descent and not by religion.

Nothing short of complete separation of state and religion with concomitant secularization of public life can satisfy this minority. The rest of the population, including that silent majority which does not participate in the periodic skirmishes of the ongoing *Kulturkampf*, longs for an easing of the tension created by this state of affairs.

Nowadays, even if judged on strict halakhic grounds, religious coercion is undesirable because it tends to be counterproductive. It may cause a revulsion from anything ritually Jewish—a fear which is of halakhic importance and deserves very careful consideration on the part of those who initiate religious ordinances meant for universal application. In times when the belief in religion was strong, the coercion practiced in Judaism may have been justified in order to help the believer overcome his innate weakness and thus serve the Lord as he really felt he ought. In times of religious doubt, however, no good can come of it.

What then can be done when state and religion are not separated to take the sting out of coercion in relation to the institution of religious laws referred to earlier in this chapter? I would like to submit the following suggestions.

1. Religious parties or other bodies that attempt to introduce an ordinance of religious import in the Knesset or local authority would be well-advised to prepare the ground carefully by ascertaining whether its adoption reflects national or local consensus. The techniques used in public opinion polls and surveys are sufficiently developed to be able to forecast popular opinion with a reasonable measure of accuracy.

2. In order to strengthen the proposed safeguards against religious coercion, the main political parties, whoever they may be, would do well to remove religious issues from the constraints of coalition discipline and allow the individual member of the Knesset to vote according to his or her conscience. With such an arrangement no firm promise could be made by the main parties that a proposal of a religious character would *a priori* be adopted. The beginning of such an arrangement can be seen with regard to the recognition by the state of non-Orthodox conversion to Judaism. A number of Likud coalition members voted with the opposition against the exclusion of other streams of Judaism, claiming that on religious matters they ought to be allowed to vote as they thought fit. And there are other examples. The general acceptance of such a rule would invalidate the reproach of negotiation under duress—the current coalition procedure. Moreover, a majority vote in the Knesset, unhampered by party considerations, may be claimed to mirror a majority consensus of the nation at large.

I am aware that even if this principle were adopted, the minority which demands a neat separation of state and religion and absolute freedom from coercion in their private lives would not be placated. But no democracy, however advanced, can satisfy the wishes of all its citizens, legitimate as they may be, just as in a democracy with a Christian majority not all the susceptibilities of Jews and Moslems could be taken into account.

The adoption of a free vote in religious matters would greatly weaken the *raison d'être* of religious parties, which in any case are in a state of decline. A more serious objection might be that in the course of time the principle of a free vote on religious issues might be instrumental in opening up the whole issue of the status quo in matters of state and religion, and produce surprising results. In a true democracy there is no alternative to relying on the good sense of the people's representatives. Though I do not favor a separation of state and religion I am bound to accept the verdict of the majority. "Leave the people of Israel in peace; though they may not be prophets yet they be sons of prophets" (*Pesachim* 66a).

3. Finally, to do away with the anomaly of nonrecognition by the state of Conservative and Reform Judaism, it would be highly desirable that the Orthodox rabbinate meet with representatives

of the modern trends in order to discuss the issue of marriage and divorce in Israel with the aim of arriving at a solution acceptable to all. I know that in view of the substantial ideological differences between the three schools of thought this is obviously easier said than done. In the first place, the Israeli Orthodox rabbinate would have to overcome deeply rooted psychological and ideological inhibitions in order to deem their counterparts in the other two streams partners worthy of cooperation. Then they would have to summon all the forces inherent in Halakhah which call for peace and unity, share the human strivings for which the House of Hillel has become famous, and activate all the *ahavat Yisrael* of which they are capable, in order to give such an encounter the maximum chance of success. As for the representatives of the modern trends, they would have to recognize that for them too there has arisen an "exigency of the hour"—*hora'at sha'ah*—which demands that they tap their own halakhic roots to the utmost so that on this vital issue an agreed solution may be found.

The change of heart required of the Orthodox has been put rather succinctly by a well-known Orthodox rabbi:

It is our conviction that halakhah has to be stretched to its limits in order to further Jewish unity and to better mutual understanding. In the Orthodox camp there are certain psychological impediments that have to be overcome. It is time that Orthodox rabbis face without dogmatism the issue of their relationship to rabbis of the non-Orthodox denominations. Judged in the light of the real situation, it is just not true that the latter, because of their Conservative or Reform interpretation of Judaism, are incapable of *Yir'at Shamayim*. To insist that this is so is a prejudice; it is insisting on an untruth that, as such, is a violation of important Biblical commandments.[11]

In view of the increased activities of the two modern streams of Judaism in Israel on one hand, and the decline of the Orthodox religious parties on the other hand, the status quo in matters of state and religion is no longer as secure as it used to be, and a severance of religion from the state may possibly materialize in the future. The time is ripe for a change in the present pattern. To foresee the fruit of an action, or for that matter of an omission, is, according to the rabbis, the height of human wisdom. Cooperation between the three streams in Judaism is the "call of the hour," as it may forestall a complete severance of state and religion. Should this cooperation materialize, it would be hailed as a breakthrough in the religious life of the state.

11

State and Religion: A Dialogue with Eliezer Berkovits

Zvi Kurzweil: Am I right in assuming that when writing your book *The Nature and Function of Halakhah* in Hebrew, and its English version, *Not in Heaven*, it was your aim to show the vitality and adaptability of Halakhah—not frozen, as it is contended. In other words you're trying to point to a number of important inherent principles which make possible its adaptability to modern conditions. Would you say that this was the main aim of the book?

Eliezer Berkovits: I would just correct one word you have used twice: adaptability. If you use this expression, you actually imply that I'm going to change something, and this wasn't my intention at all. I believe that I was trying to show that it is not a question of adapting Halakhah but applying it to changing situations. Of its very essence it must be capable of dealing with any actual situation that arises at any time in the life of the Jewish people. What we have to do is to establish what those principles are and apply them to conditions which have arisen. I want to give you an example: you know in Israel some time ago there arose the problem of autopsy, and the halakhic decisions on this problem were to a large extent based on a responsum of the *Noda be-Yehuda* (Rabbi Ezekiel Landau, the famous eighteenth-century rabbinic scholar), who was the rabbi of the Jewish community of

Prague. It is obvious that his responsum was related to a Jewish minority living in non-Jewish surroundings. It may be taken for granted that from time to time Jewish persons had to be hospitalized, possibly also in institutions other than those of their own community. How can Rabbi Landau's responsum serve as a model for our situation in Israel, where the Jewish state is responsible for the entire health service and concomitant medical sciences?

Zvi Kurzweil: But are you confident that problems arising in such a different setting, within a sovereign Jewish state, which previous halakhic authorities never imagined, not envisioning the emergence of a Jewish state in their lifetime, or in later generations, can be tackled by halakhic means? Since this was beyond their imagination, they could not have pondered such questions as the maintenance of essential service on Shabbat and festivals.

Eliezer Berkovits: I have to say that it can be done on the classical principles of Halakhah, and that is why I have endeavored to formulate them in a way they are not usually seen, and in the English version of my book you will find a certain indication as to how they can be applied to a modern democratic state. I must make the assumption that it can be done, that halakhic principles can be applied to the solution of any problem arising in any situation, including those within an independent Jewish state. Were I not to believe that the Torah wants the Jewish people to live in *Erez. Yisrael,* I would have to agree with Neturei Karta that our place is in the Diaspora, where we have to wait until the coming of the Messiah. I cannot accept this, for I cannot believe that there is a divinely ordained design for the Jewish people to live in the Galut. So as a matter of principle—perhaps one of the most important—I must assume that Halakhah is applicable to day-to-day life in a Jewish state.

Zvi Kurzweil: Once you adopt this attitude, the question of state legislation in religious matters intended for a highly heterogeneous population arises: the Shabbat-observance law, the marriage and divorce laws, the law pertaining to autopsies, etc. In the Galut there is the possibility of creating different Jewish communities answering to differing ideas and susceptibilities; in other words, you have religious pluralism. Here in Israel you have a number of religious laws which apply to all, no matter what their religious convictions. I want to ask you if you accept this situation as desirable; to put it briefly, are you in favor of state legislation in matters of Halakhah?

Eliezer Berkovits: No, I am not. You know, some time ago I published an article in *Ma'ariv* about whether religious coercion is justified from the point of view of Halakhah. It is my thesis that it is not. Please don't misunderstand me. In principle, the state and religion are of course not separable, but in actual fact we cannot establish halakhic authority without the ancient institution of *semikhah* and the Sanhedrin. In the absence of these, the halakhic authority of the time has to be freely accepted by the people for whom it legislates, and this, unfortunately, is not the case if you consider the Israeli population as a whole.

As far as state legislation in matters of religion goes, the Knesset is, of course, not to be viewed as a halakhic authority. It is secular state authority. So the question arises: how does Halakhah view state authority? There are two possibilities. It is either in the nature of *mishpat ha-melekh* ("the law of the king"), supplementing the ordinary halakhic system; or it is similar to non-Jewish state authority, which is also binding on Jews provided that it is not discriminatory and does not legislate in matters of religion. *Mishpat ha-melekh* does not apply to the Knesset; we have no prophet and no Sanhedrin to appoint a king, so we cannot invest the Knesset with quasi-royal authority. So we are left with the second alternative, which certainly applies, but only in secular matters, such as taxation, army service, criminal law, etc., but not in matters of religion.

Zvi Kurzweil: I understand from what you are saying that you would not object if the Knesset were to abrogate the Law of Marriage and Divorce and make civil marriage possible. And what about the other religious laws? You would not mind if they too were repealed?

Eliezer Berkovits: I go further. I maintain that on halakhic grounds the Knesset has no right to institute and enforce religious laws, and the fact that it does so, does not help Judaism. On the contrary, I believe it does harm. Let me comment on the marriage ceremony. For many Israelis it is meaningless, some even make fun of it. Were they to enter into civil marriages, it would be much better, because halakhically speaking this would not have the validity of changing their personal status from single to married, with all the far-reaching consequences flowing from this. Those who do not accept halakhic Judaism are prone to engage in all sorts of practices viewed by Halakhah as immoral (such as exchanging wives, etc.), and this may result in illegitimate offspring—*mamzerut*. Only those who accept halakhic Judaism should marry *kedat Moshe ve-Yisrael*. Those who are forced by the law of the state to stand under a *chupah*, which they would not have done of their own free choice, had better marry civilly. Moreover, the very act of compulsion in religious matters is objectionable. In matters of the spirit you cannot achieve anything by coercion. It does not command respect, it is harmful. As for the other religious laws, they could also be dispensed with, except, of course, Kashrut, limited Shabbat laws, and recognition of the Jewish festivals.

Zvi Kurzweil: You know, Rabbi Berkovits, you are now treading on very controversial ground. There are two points I should like to make. First of all, social conditions here are quite different from those in the United States. In matters of sexual relationships, Israel is less permissive than the United States, which has been proven by a number of researches. We have to bear in mind that the majority of the Israeli population is of oriental origin, and these Jews do not know of any other way of getting married than the traditional Jewish one. You may be influenced by the lack of decorum obtaining in the course of marriage ceremonies here in Israel, but this lack of decorum, regrettable though it is, does not reflect upon their regard for the seriousness and solemnity of the occasion, though this contention of mine may seem paradoxical to you. Secondly, the halakhic attitude of the Israeli rabbinate—including all present and past Chief Rabbis—as well as authorities such as the *Chazon Ish*, take a more serious attitude of the validity of civil marriage than you do. I have read a letter of the *Chazon Ish* on this point, and he makes it clear that the dissolution of a civil marriage requires a Jewish bill of divorce, as well as the usual interval of three months for the wife before entering a second marriage. I do not want to go into halakhic technicalities, but let me say this: here in Israel even a civil marriage is viewed by the rabbis as a contractual undertaking of both partners motivated by a desire for legality and social approval. This being so, the institution of civil marriage—and not its nonoccurrence, as you claim—would create serious problems, for civil marriage, if broken up, is usually dissolved by civil authorities, and the halakhic consequences then are obvious—the danger of *mamzerut*. Moreover, marriage with *chupa* and *kiddushin* tends to strengthen the historical consciousness of our people and works for unity. Also, the contact with the Israeli rabbi prior to marriage exercises a beneficial moral influence. In short, I believe that your opinion on this important issue is strongly influenced by your American background, and you do not seem to take into account the entirely different Israeli situation.

Eliezer Berkovits: The fact that the majority of the Israeli population, being of oriental origin, knows no other way of getting married than the traditional Jewish one can, of course, have no influence on my positon. For if so, they will continue to get married *kedat Moshe ve-Yisrael* even if civil marriage were introduced.

As to the halakhically binding nature of a civil marriage, it is a very serious subject that cannot be treated in this discussion. The position of those who think that it is, is not unknown to me. In America I am inclined to look at it sympathetically (please, do not take this as my final opinion). However, the halakhic significance of civil marriage changes fundamentally when one deals with people who, as a matter of principle and conviction, reject the very idea of *kedat Moshe ve-Yisrael*.

Be that as it may, however complicated the situation arising may be, the halakhic rule retains its validity that Halakhah does not recognize the authority of the state to legislate halakhically.

Neither do I believe that the present situation is conducive to unity. In matters of the spirit, especially concerning religious convictions, compulsion is counterproductive. It is resented and it alienates. What is left is the way of persuasion. It is, of course, much more difficult a task than politically produced legislation. But it is also much more hopeful and worthwhile.

12

Postscript

Some further observations on the concept of Neo-Orthodoxy may be called for. In the first chapter I have dwelt on Mendelssohn's positive attitude toward the emancipation of Jews, although it was not without painful heart-searching and doubts as to the risk involved. Because of his insistence on Halakhah in the traditional sense, Mendelssohn cannot be classified as a Reform Jew. Neo-Orthodoxy as a movement is also diametrically opposed to the movement for Reform, which, from its beginning, rejected the principle of *Torah min ha-shamayim* and aimed at changing Halakhah in a fundamental sense, as well as the traditional Jewish liturgy, attempting to make them more amenable to the spirit of their non-Jewish environment.

Nowadays, the emancipation of Jews is an accepted fact in the free world. Reform Judaism has also become a fact, and there is no longer a polemic of a theological nature beween the two trends. Hence it is no longer meaningful to characterize Neo-Orthodoxy by its positive attitude toward emancipation, which is no longer an issue, or for that matter by its opposition to Reform Judaism, which it shares with the old Orthodoxy.

I have pointed out that the main characteristic of Neo-Ortho-doxy is its openness in an intellectual sense, its belief in the possibility of synthesis between Judaism and universal culture. I have also noted that according to Samson Raphael Hirsch the

Orthodox Jew's involvement in general culture is not only permissible and legitimate from a religious point of view, but even desirable, inasmuch as it brings about an enrichment of personality, not to mention the social and economic advantages accruing from a comprehensive and many-sided education.

This turning to the non-Jewish intellectual world naturally leads to a reflection about the specific traits of Judaism on the one hand, and the spiritual strivings and aspirations common to Jew and gentile. In other words, this widening of outlook helps to draw attention to the national as distinct from the universal aspects of Judaism. This is the reason why I have included a chapter on the philosophy of Rabbi Soloveitchik, in which I find the universal tendency clearly articulated.

I do not believe that Neo-Orthodoxy or, for that matter, even the old-type Orthodoxy, may be aptly characterized as fundamentalist. The concepts of fundamentalism were better relegated to the Christian context from which it has sprung. Any student versed in the Talmud knows that the rabbis dealt with Scripture in a quasi-autonomous manner, that is to say, in accordance with a well-defined set of hermeneutic principles of interpretation handed down by oral tradition. The Torah itself authorizes them to do so, stating expressly in Deuteronomy 17:11, "according to the sentence of the law which they [i.e., the rabbis] shall teach thee, and according to the judgment which they shall tell thee, thou shalt do: thou shalt not decline from the sentence which they shall show thee, neither to the right nor to the left." The only sect in Judaism that may rightly be termed fundamentalist is that of the Karaites, and it is no mere accident that this religious sect did not survive in any significant manner.

The chapter on "*Torah min ha-Shamayim* in Neo-Orthodox Perspective" is not intended to suggest that the ideas of the philosophers dealt with in this chapter are unquestioningly accepted by other representative Neo-Orthodox thinkers. The opposite is closer to the truth. What is characteristic of Neo-Orthodox thought, and I hope clearly brought out in that chapter, is the courageous attempt to confront the theories of higher criticism and dispute their conclusions, without shrinking from what is involved in such a confrontation. I have called this tendency agonistic. It is prompted by the exhortation of the sages: "Know what answer to give the unbeliever."

The problems of religious freedom in Israel, the status of women in Judaism, and the relation between state and religion are issues of deep concern to the modern Orthodox Jew. Their solution is necessary both in the interests of Neo-Orthodoxy per se, as well as for its harmonious coexistence with the non-Orthodox sections of the community.

Naturally, we do not find all the traits of Neo-Orthodoxy elaborated in this essay in one thinker alone; often a philosopher who may be termed Neo-Orthodox also exhibits leanings toward the old-type Orthodoxy. Finally, there may be Orthodox thinkers who defy ready categorization. In broad generalization, I would say that the Neo-Orthodox, though cleaving to Halakhah in an immanent sense, form a bridge to the secular majority of Jews, striving to maintain the fundamental unity of Jewry. While marching with the times, they use the art of Torah interpretation as a legitimate strategy in solving problems engendered by conflicts between tradition and the modern exigencies of life.

Footnotes Chapter 1

NOTES

1. Moses Mendelssohn, *Jerusalem* (Berlin: Welt Verlag, 1919), p. 37.
2. Ibid., p. 64.
3. Ibid., p. 115.
4. Ibid., p. 66.
5. A similar situation is described by Yaacov Herzog: "It is told of Baron Nathaniel Rothschild that, after winning his battle of many years to have the disabilities to members of the Jewish faith removed from the House of Lords, he slipped away from the hierarchy of Britain congratulating him on the achievement and was to be found prostrate in prayer in a small synagogue in the Whitechapel ghetto of East London, his lips murmuring, 'Would that this freedom shall not mean the diminution of our faith.' " Yaacov Herzog, *A People That Dwells Alone* (London: Weidenfeld & Nicolson, 1976), p. 145.
6. *Jerusalem*, p. 81.
7. Ibid., p. 69.
8. Alexander Altmann, *Moses Mendelssohn: A Biographical Study* (University, Ala.: University of Alabama Press, 1973), p. 547.
9. Yitzhak Heinemann, *Ta'amei ha-Mitzvot be-Sifrut Yisrael* (Jerusalem, 1955).
10. Sa'adia Gaon, *The Book of Beliefs and Opinions,* translated from the Arabic and the Hebrew by Samuel Rosenblatt (New Haven: Yale University Press, 1967), p. 163.
11. Ibid., p. 14.
12. Yaacov Levinger, "Shelemut Enoshit etzel ha-Goyim le'fi ha-Rambam," in *Hagut* (Jerusalem, 1978), p. 35.
13. See below, Chapter 2.
14. Nathan Rotenstreich's introduction to *Jerusalem* (Ramat-Gan: Massada, 1947), p. 30.
15. Heinrich Heine, *Sämtliche Schriften,* vol. 3 (Munich: Carl Hanser Verlag, 1971), pp. 584–585; see also Heinz Knobloch, *Herr Moses in Berlin* (Buchverlag Der Morgen, 1979), p. 392.

Footnotes Chapter 2

NOTES

1. Samson Raphael Hirsch, *Judaism Eternal,* ed. Rabbi I. Grunfeld (London: Soncino Press, 1958).

2. S. R. Hirsch, *The Nineteen Letters of Ben Uziel,* trans. Dr. B. Drachman, (New York: Bloch Publishing Co., 1899).

3. *Deoth,* no. 40, 1959.

4. Max Wiener, *Die Jüdische Religion im Zeitalter der Emanzipation* (Berlin: Philo Verlag, 1933), p. 7.

5. Nathan Rotenstreich, *Ha-Machshavah ha-Yehudit B'eit ha-Chadashah* (Tel-Aviv: Am Oved, 1945), vol. I, p. 115.

6. Abraham Geiger, *Leben und Lebenswerk, von Ludwig Geiger* (Berlin: Verl. Georg Reiner, 1910), p. 292.

7. Hirsch, *Nineteen Letters of Ben Uziel,* pp. 190–191.

8. Ibid., pp. 181–183.

9. *The Seventy-Fifth Anniversary Book of the Hirsch School (Festschrift zum 75 jährigen Bestehen der Realschule mit Lyzeum der isr. Religionsgesellschaft)* (Frankfurt a. Main: Herman Verlag, 1928), pp. 160 ff.

10. Geiger, op. cit., p. 11.

11. Grunfeld, introduction to Hirsch, *Judaism Eternal,* vol. I, pp. 26–27.

Footnotes Chapter 3

NOTES

1. Isaac Breuer, *Concepts of Judaism,* selected and edited by Jacob S. Levinger (Jerusalem: Israel Universities Press, 1974).

2. *Der Neue Kusari* (Frankfurt am Main: Verlag der Rabbiner Hirsch Gesellschaft, 1934), p. 80.

3. Ibid.

4. Isaac Breuer, *Programm oder Testament* (Frankfurt am Main: J. Kaufmann Verlag, 1929), p. 57.

5. *Der Neue Kusari,* p. 81.

6. Ibid., pp. 87–88.

7. Ibid., p. 393.

8. "Politik der Mystik, zu Isaac Breuer's *Neue Kusari,*" July 17, 1934.

9. In his article "Science, Natural Law and Ethics" (published in *Ethics in an Age of Pervasive Technology,* ed. Melvin Kranzberg [Boul-

der, Col.: Westview Press], p. 90), Robert Gordis quotes John Cogley's
definition of natural law as "simply the belief that there is a moral order
or ethical order which a human being can discover and which he must
take account of, if he is to attune himself to his necessary ends as a
human being."

10. *Guardians of Our Heritage* (New York: Bloch Publishing Company, 1958), p. 628.

11. Ibid., p. 634.

12. M. Rosenfeld: *H. P. Chajes* (Vienna, 1933), pp. 171–172.

13. It may be objected that Breuer and Chajes argued from different
presuppositions (though Chajes, too, characterizes himself as a Torah-
true Jew), and hence Chajes's criticism of Breuer may not be valid.
Nevertheless, Rabbi Chajes's protest against the very conception of
"sovereignty of Torah" seems justified. Even if it is conceded to Breuer
that the Jewish people as a whole have forefeited their "sovereignty"
because of their allegiance to Torah, sworn on Sinai, at least their sages
may still be regarded as "sovereign," since the interpretation of Torah is
entrusted to them.

14. *Guardians of Our Heritage,* p. 625.

15. Kurt Blumenfeld, *Erlebte Judenfrage* (Stuttgart: Deutsche
Verlagsanstalt, 1962), p. 171; see also Yehuda Kurt Blumenfeld, *She'elat
ha-Yehudiam Kehavaya* (Jerusalem: Ha-Sifriah ha-Zionit, 1963).

Footnotes Chapter 4

NOTES

1. *Daedalus,* Winter 1982, p. 23.

2. *Yahadut, Am Yehudi, u-Medinat Yisrael* (Tel-Aviv: Schocken,
1976), p. 26.

3. *Emunah, Historiah ve-Arakhim* (Tel-Aviv: Akademon, 1982), p.
144.

4. *Yahadut, Am Yehudi u-Medinat Yisrael,* p. 340.

5. Ibid.

6. The *Jerusalem Post* of June 11, 1982, quotes Leibowitz as saying:
"I said civil war is not the worst thing that can happen. Of all wars, civil
wars are the only ones that are worthwhile, which you never can say
about wars between nations, because only civil wars are fought for
values."

7. *Yahadut, Am Yehudi u-Medinat Yisrael,* p. 177.

8. See J. J. Ross, "Antropotzentrism Ve-theotzentrism," *Sefer J.
Leibowitz* (Agudat ha-Studentim, University of Tel-Aviv, 1977), p. 56.

Footnotes Chapter 5

NOTES

1. Norman Lamm, *Faith and Doubt*, (New York: KTAV Publishing House, 1971).

2. Sa'adia, *The Book of Doctrines and Beliefs*, translated and edited by Alexander Altmann (London: East and West Library, 1946), p. 33.

3. Isaac Breuer, *Concepts of Judaism*, selected and edited by Jacob S. Levinger (Jerusalem: Israel Universities Press, 1974), p. 48.

4. Ibid., p. 46.

5. Ibid.

6. Ibid., p. 52.

7. Lamm, op. cit., p. 6.

8. Richard R. Niebuhr, *Experimental Religion* (New York: Harper & Row, 1972), p. 14.

9. Emanuel Rackman, *One Man's Judaism* (New York: Philosophical Library, 1970), p. 17.

10. It is interesting to note in this context that Isaac Breuer called the Jewish Orthodoxy of his time *Dennoch-Orthodoxie*, i.e., "Orthodoxy in spite of."

11. Paul Tillich, *Dynamics of Faith* (New York: Harper & Brothers, 1957), pp. 21–22.

12. Mordecai Cohen, "Al ha-Safek," *Petachim*, March 1980.

13. Ibid., p. 47.

14. Arthur Green, *Tormented Master: A Life of Rabbi Nachman of Bratslav* (University, Ala.: University of Alabama Press, 1979), p. 291.

15. Ibid., p. 292.

16. Ibid., p. 306.

17. Eliezer Berkovits, *Faith after the Holocaust* (New York: KTAV Publishing House, 1973), p. 129.

18. In his commentary to the Hebrew prayer book, pt. I, p. 327.

Footnotes Chapter 6

NOTES

1. Isaac Breuer, *Der Neue Kusari* (Frankfurt am Main: Verlag der Rabbiner Hirsch Gesellschaft, 1934), p. 337.

2. Professor J. Tishbi of the Hebrew University attempted to trace the historical development of the God-Torah-Israel "trio" in a learned article published in the bibliographic journal *Kiryat Sefer*, vol. 50, pp. 180–192. He mentions, among other sources, Rabbi J. Horowitz's kabbalistic

treatise *Two Tablets of Stone*, in which the "trio" occurs in a fairly clearly crystallized fashion. Isaac Breuer is known to have immersed himself in the study of this work; hence it is very likely that he derived the formula from it. Tishbi claims that the most precise formulation of the concept God-Torah-Israel was made by Rabbi Moshe Haim Luzzatto in the eighteenth century. According to Tishbi's conjecture it appeared first in 1731.

3. M. Breuer, "Emunah u-Madda^c be-Parshanut ha-Miqra," *Deot*, Fall 1953 and Winter 1960.

4. See Denis Donoghue, 1982 Reith Lecture V, *The Listener*, December 9, 1982.

5. Avraham Isaac Kook, *Orot ha-Kodesh*, vol. II (Jerusalem: Mosad ha-Rav Kook, 1964), p. 547.

6. Avraham Isaac Kook, *Igrot*, vol. I (Jerusalem: Mosad ha-Rav Kook, 1964), p. 164.

7. Z. R. Werblowsky, "Madda haMikra keBa'yah datit," *Molad* 18 (1960): 162–168.

8. Professor Yehuda T. Radday of the Technion's General Studies Department, with the help of an Israeli team and a German scientist, has used the most modern statistical methods to check upon Wellhausen, who attributes the Book of Genesis to three authors. This recent research suggests that the traditionalists may have been correct and Genesis has but one author. The team used a combination of statistics, linguistics, and computer science in connection with biblical scholarship. The 20,000 words of the Book of Genesis were analyzed according to fifty-four criteria, including word length, the use of the definite article and the conjunction *and*, richness of vocabulary, and transition frequencies between word categories. Such criteria are held by the researchers to be a reliable gauge of authorship because such traits are not only countable but also beyond the author's control.

9. The tolerant attitude of Hayim Hirschensohn, an American Orthodox rabbi, to academic Bible research, including higher criticism, might be mentioned here. In his halakhic treatise *Malki ba-Kodesh*, he establishes a graded scale of halakhically permissible or forbidden activities. To deny the Mosaic authorship of the Bible, or to admit it while maintaining that Moses was not divinely inspired, is tantamount to heresy. However, these are the only absolute "thou shalt nots" as regards Bible research. Any other relevant scholarly approach, be it archaeological, historical, philological, or exegetic in a general sense, as well as the suggestion of changes in the masoretic text of the Bible, is either unconditionally permitted or permitted within the framework of university studies, though not encouraged. The motive for leniency in this

matter is "in order to know what to answer the heretic." *Malki ba-Kodesh*, pt. 2 (New York: Moinester Printing Co., 5681), pp. 243–250.

10. Gershom Scholem, *Major Trends in Jewish Mysticism* (New York: Schocken Books, 1961), p. 18.

11. Yeshayahu Leibowitz, *Yahadut, Am Yehudi u-Medinat Yisrael* (Tel Aviv: Schocken, 1976), p. 348.

12. G. Weiler, "Emet Ve-Ezrachut," in *Sefer Yeshayahu Leibowitz* (Tel-Aviv University, 1978), p. 101.

13. D. Weiss-Halivni's attempt to make use of the Lurian kabbalistic concept of *zimzum* in relation to the written text of Torah appears to be more in the nature of a reaction to the moral problems it poses than to higher criticism and academic biblical scholarship in general. He believes that a text which emanates from the divine may contain deficiencies: "The Divine, for unfathomable reasons, chose as it were to reveal a less than perfect Torah, allowing erring man to introduce corruption and misunderstanding. . . . He created man with an enormous potential for evil, permitting him to follow his own moral inclinations. . . . Why then should we expect of Him to have acted so differently in relation to the Torah? Why should He have given man a perfect instrument, enabling him to reach the greatest of heights without concomitantly making it liable to his corruptive tendencies?" David Weiss Halivni, "Revelation and *Zimzum*," *Judaism* 21, no. 2 (Spring 1972).

Footnotes Chapter 7

NOTES

1. Joseph B. Soloveitchik, "The Lonely Man of Faith," *Tradition* 7, no. 2 (Summer 1965): 12.

2. Ibid., p. 14.

3. Ibid., p. 16.

4. Ibid., p. 24.

5. Ibid.

6. Ibid., p. 44.

7. Ibid., p. 57.

8. Ibid., p. 59.

9. *Ish ha-Halakhah—Galuj ve-Nistar* (Jerusalem: World Zionist Organization, 1979), p. 91.

10. Ibid., p. 101.

11. Ibid., p. 90.

12. Ibid., p. 53.

13. *Al ha-Teshuvah*, collected and edited by Pinhas H. Peli (Torah Education Department of the World Zionist Organization, 1974).

14. *Ish ha-Halakhah*, p. 14.
15. Ibid., p. 72.
16. Ibid., p. 73.
17. Ibid., p. 11.
18. Ibid., p. 105.
19. It is interesting to note that the same distinction, but with different variations, has been adopted by a number of philosophers and social scientists. I recall William Whyte's "organization man," largely shaped by the industrial establishment, Herbert Marcuse's "one-dimensional man," devoid of originality and spontaneity, influenced to an alarming extent by the communication media, and the outer-directed man of David Riesman (*The Lonely Crowd*), who is activated by the conventions accepted by his environment, rather than deriving orientation from inner feelings and convictions.
20. *Ish ha-Halakhah*, p. 107.
21. Ibid., p. 84.
22. Translated into the Hebrew as "Beit ha-Knesset Mossad ve-Rayon," in *Divrei Hagut ve-ha'arakha* (World Zionist Organization, 1981), pp. 99–116.
23. John Macquarrie, *An Existentialist Theology* (New York: Penguin Books, 1980), p. 68.

Footnotes Chapter 8

NOTES

1. There is a chronological discrepancy in this story, for Yehoshua ben Perakhia lived about a hundred years before Jesus. See Tractate *Sotah*, p. 47a.
2. Ephraim E. Urbach, *The Sages* (Jerusalem: Magnes Press, Hebrew University, 1975), p. 639.
3. Abraham Isaac Kook, *Igrot*, vol. I (Jerusalem: Mossad ha-Rav Kook, 1961), pp. 369–370.
4. Ibid., pp. 369–370.
5. *Hazon ha-Geulah* (Brooklyn, 1974), p. 110.

Footnotes Chapter 9

NOTES

1. Yeshayahu Leibowitz, *Emunah, Historiah ve-Arakhim* (Jerusalem: Akademon, 1982), p. 72.
2. Ibid., p. 73.

3. Ze'ev Falk, *Erchei Misphat ve-Yahadut* (Jerusalem: Magnes Press, Hebrew University, 1980), p. 171.

4. *The Jewish Woman in Responsa Literature,* included in the Jewish Library, Third Series, edited by Rabbi Leo Jung (Jewish Library Publishing Co., 1934).

Footnotes Chapter 10

NOTES

1. Karel Čapek, *Hovory s T.G. Masarykem* (Prague: Borový-Čin, (1937), pp. 300–301.

2. Mayer Sulzberger, *The Am Ha-Arez: The Ancient Hebrew Parliament* (Philadelphia, 1909), pp. 76–78.

3. Ibid.

4. Under the headline "The Chill Factor," the *Jerusalem Post* (March 21, 1983) reports upon the poll conducted by Dr. Mina Zemach of Dahaf showing that over one-third of all Israelis would prefer a nondemocratic form of government, or at least a form in which leaders are independent of political parties. In an editorial, the *Jerusalem Post* comments: "The Dahaf poll is cause for deepest worry, for a democracy that is not backed by the overwhelming majority of the people cannot long expect to remain free." This may sound rather gloomy, for we do not know to what extent the results of a poll, taken only once—in a political situation which happens to display some ugly features of an "unbridled democracy"— should be taken at their face value; it may have been influenced by the unsavory phenomenon of political haggling taking place within a multi-party coalition government. Nor do we know what was really in the minds of the people who so lightly expressed themselves in favor of a nondemocratic regime. They may possibly have cast a nostalgic look upon Zionist leaders such as Herzl, Weizmann, and Ben-Gurion, harking back to the paternal character of their leadership. However this may be, the fact remains that even if we accept the pessimistic results of the Dahaf poll, almost two-thirds of the Israeli population expressed themselves as in favor of democracy.

5. See Peter Koslowski, "Über die Grenzen staatlicher Fürsorge hinaus," *Frankfurter Allgemeine Zeitung,* July 2, 1983.

6. Yaacov Herzog, *A People That Dwells Alone* (London: Weidenfeld & Nicolson, 1976), p. 162.

7. Nathan Rotenstreich, "Secularism and Religion in Israel," *Judaism* 15 (1966): 262.

8. Herzog, op. cit., p. 162.

9. According to Professor Uriel Schwartz of the Hebrew University (in a research paper sponsored by the London Institute for Jewish Affairs) by the year 2000, Diaspora Jewry will shrink by 20 to 25 percent whereas the Jewish population of Israel will grow to 4.5 million. See *Ha'arez*, May 15, 1983.

10. See Oswald Rufeisen, "Neged Sar ha-P'nim," in *Ba'im ke-Echad* by Moshe Silberg, (Jerusalem: Magnes Press, Hebrew University, 1981), pp. 381 ff.

11. Eliezer Berkovits, *Not in Heaven* (New York: KTAV Publishing House, 1983), p. 107.